Jim,
I hope you
enjoy my little
book!

Bart Lencioni

Praise for Patrick Lencioni's
The Five Temptations of a CEO

"The most fascinating book I have ever read about management."

   —**Tadao Kobayashi,** executive vice president, American Honda Motor Company

"Not since reading *The Seven Habits of Highly Effective People* have I been so inspired. I have a feeling I will be frequently sharing your book with others."

   —**Micahel F. Pandich, Jr.,** senior vice president, sales, United Asset Coverage, Inc.

"A must-read for all leaders, not just CEOs. Take it from someone who has been tempted. Better than a personal coach."

   —**Boyd Clarke,** president and CEO, The Tom Peters Group

"There are few books that I have come across that strike at the heart of the challenges of leading an organization better than *The Five Temptations of a CEO*. Patrick Lencioni has hit a home run in crafting a message that is engaging and to the point."

   —**John Vitale,** director, human resources, PerkinElmer Instruments

"I read it on vacation and could not put it down. I look forward to providing a copy of this to all the CEOs in our portfolio."

—**Rick Patch,** partner, Sequel Venture Partners

The Four
Obsessions of an
Extraordinary
Executive

The Four Obsessions of an Extraordinary Executive

A Leadership Fable

Patrick Lencioni

Author of *The Five Temptations of a CEO*

JOSSEY-BASS
A Wiley Company
San Francisco

Published by

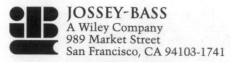

JOSSEY-BASS
A Wiley Company
989 Market Street
San Francisco, CA 94103-1741

www.josseybass.com

Copyright © 2000 by Patrick Lencioni.

Jossey-Bass is a registered trademark of John Wiley & Sons, Inc.

Jossey-Bass books and products are available through most bookstores. To
contact Jossey-Bass directly, call (888) 378-2537, fax to (800) 605-2665, or
visit our website at www.josseybass.com.

Substantial discounts on bulk quantities of Jossey-Bass books are available
to corporations, professional associations, and other organizations. For
details and discount information, contact the special sales department at
Jossey-Bass.

We at Jossey-Bass strive to use the most environmentally sensitive paper stocks
available to us. Our publications are printed on acid-free recycled stock whenever
possible, and our paper always meets or exceeds minimum GPO and EPA
requirements.

Library of Congress Cataloging-in-Publication Data
Lencioni, Patrick, 1965-
    The four obsessions of an extraordinary executive: a leadership fable /
Patrick Lencioni.—1st ed.
        p. cm.
ISBN 0-7879-5403-9 (acid-free paper)
    1. Executives—Fiction. I. Title.
    HD38.2 .L46 2000
    658.4'09—dc21   00-009560

FIRST EDITION
HB Printing   10 9 8 7

CONTENTS

Contents

For Joel, a coach and a leader through and through
(1959-1983)

THE FOUR OBSESSIONS OF AN EXTRAORDINARY EXECUTIVE

Rich O'Connor's detractors said he was lucky. Others believed he had a natural gift for management and leadership.

Little did they know.

INTRODUCTION

If everything is important, then nothing is.

No one understands the power of this saying more than a person who leads an organization. Whether it is a multinational corporation, a department within a larger company, or a small entrepreneurial venture, every organization provides its leader with more distractions and concerns than one person can handle.

The key to managing this challenge, of course, is to identify a reasonable number of issues that will have the greatest possible impact on the success of your organization, and then spend most of your time thinking about, talking about, and working on those issues.

But what are they? Before we can identify them, it is important to understand what is ultimately necessary for organizational success.

I believe that all successful organizations share two qualities: they are smart, and they are healthy. An organization demonstrates that it is smart by developing intelligent strategies, marketing plans, product features, and financial models that lead to competitive advantage over its rivals. It demonstrates that it is healthy by eliminating politics and confusion, which leads to higher morale, lower turnover, and higher productivity.

As important as both of these topics are, I have found that most leaders spend the majority of their time and energy making their organizations smarter, with relatively little effort directed toward making them healthier. This is understandable considering the predominant focus of business schools and business media. It is regrettable, however, when one considers the powerful and unique attributes of organizational health.

First, healthy organizations have a way of making themselves smarter. Even if their ideas are temporarily inferior to those of competitors, they are usually humble and efficient enough to recognize their deficiencies and make changes in their plans before it is too late. On the other hand, plenty of anonymous and forgotten companies have squandered intellectual advantages because of infighting, lack of clarity, and other problems that plague unhealthy organizations.

Second, healthy companies are far less susceptible to ordinary problems than unhealthy ones. During difficult times, for instance, employees will remain committed to a healthy organization and stay with it longer, ultimately working to reestablish competitive advantage.

Finally—and this point is critical—no one but the head of an organization can make it healthy. While executives often successfully delegate responsibility for strategy, technology, marketing, or finance to their direct reports, they cannot assign responsibility for their organization's cultural well-being to anyone but themselves.

And so, as odd as it may seem, it is actually more important for leaders to focus on making their organizations healthy than on making them smart.

But don't misunderstand me. Not for a second am I saying that issues like strategy, product innovation, and marketing are unimportant. They are indeed critical and deserve a great deal of mindfulness from any executive team. It's just that these topics receive a wildly disproportionate amount of attention from well-meaning and intelligent executives who somehow cannot find the time and energy to focus on making their organizations healthy.

Why does this happen? Because organizational health is relatively hard to measure, and even harder to achieve. It feels soft to executives who prefer more quantitative and reliable methods of steering their companies. It also entails a longer lead time to implementation than does a technical or marketing strategy, which yields more immediate results and gratification.

But perhaps most important of all, organizational health is often neglected because it involves facing realities of human behavior that even the most committed executive is tempted to avoid. It requires levels of discipline and courage that only a truly extraordinary executive is willing to embrace.

The purpose of this book is to help executives understand the disarming simplicity and power of organizational health and the four actionable steps that allow them to achieve it. It begins with a tale of two companies, a healthy one fighting off a potential virus, and an unhealthy one searching desperately for the cure.

This is a work of fiction. Any resemblance to real life is purely unavoidable.

The Four Obsessions of an Extraordinary Executive

PART ONE

Green's Pain

THE RIVAL

⬯

Eighty million dollars in annual revenue should have made him happy. Or at least not bitter. But Vince Green, the founder and CEO of Greenwich Consulting, would not be satisfied until his company was recognized as the number one technical consulting firm in the Bay Area. And on particularly bad days, he joked that he would be truly happy only when his competitor, Telegraph Partners, was dead.

It wasn't that Telegraph was much larger than Greenwich. In fact, from time to time Greenwich rivaled Telegraph's quarterly revenue (although its profits never seemed to do so).

More than the financial war, it bothered Vince and his staff that Greenwich couldn't seem to win any of the less tangible battles. Telegraph was always regarded as a darling of the trade press. Industry analysts fawned over them. Telegraph's clients raved about their services and even stood by them during difficult times. Though Greenwich certainly garnered its share of new business, retaining clients felt like a constant struggle. On the other hand, life seemed too easy for Telegraph.

And if this bothered Vince, then the battle for employees enraged him. Telegraph didn't have to work as hard or spend as much money recruiting good people. To make matters worse, there seemed to be a small but steady stream of employees leaving Greenwich to join Telegraph, but rarely did traffic flow in the other direction. And in those few instances when employees actually did leave Telegraph for Greenwich pastures, they rarely stayed more than a year.

Perhaps the most subtle but frustrating aspect of the competitive relationship that kept Greenwich executives awake and angry at night was the fact that Telegraph's CEO, Rich O'Connor, rarely, if ever, acknowledged Greenwich. Not during press interviews, conference speeches, or client presentations. And when a Greenwich executive occasionally met Telegraph's chief executive during an industry event, almost without fail he seemed genuinely disinterested in Greenwich and unaware of what his largest and most direct competitor was doing.

All of this would have been less frustrating had Greenwich not invested so much time and money learning about its rival. From interviews with former Telegraph employees to minor acts of legal corporate espionage, Greenwich had amassed as much knowledge about its competitor as about any of its own clients.

Still, none of the surveillance yielded anything that Greenwich could put to use.

Until now.

RECONNAISSANCE

As part of his desire to understand the mystery of Telegraph's success, Vince Green occasionally invited business scholars to his staff meetings. Strategy experts, marketing professors, and finance gurus had analyzed Telegraph's practices, paying particular attention to any areas where Telegraph and Greenwich differed.

Much to the dismay of Green and his team, these experts usually found little real difference between the rival firms' business strategies. Both companies recruited from the same schools; they paid their employees similar salaries (Greenwich actually paid slightly more); they invested roughly equal amounts of money in marketing; the financial models they used to run their businesses were remarkably similar; even the prices they charged clients and the services they offered were almost identical.

Confounded by the lack of insight gained from these high-priced analysts, Green reluctantly agreed to have a local organizational development professor and consultant compare the cultures of the two companies. On the day that she came to present her findings at the weekly executive staff meeting, Green was in no mood to listen to psychobabble about the importance of employee picnics and holiday parties. He would be pleasantly surprised.

The consultant immediately grabbed the attention of everyone seated around the conference table: "Based on the information available and the research I've done, there is so little in common between Greenwich and Telegraph that making a comparison is extremely difficult."

Amazed by the apparent ridiculousness of the remark, Green was on the verge of bringing the presentation to an early halt. But before he could do so, she continued: "Something about Telegraph's culture is remarkable, like none I've ever seen. Their ability to attract clients and employees, to retain clients and employees, and even to maintain a loyal base of former clients and employees is really very impressive."

The Greenwich team was caught between two strong emotions: a sense of relief at having finally discovered even a kernel of insight that might help them understand Telegraph, and a wave of disappointment that their competitor had recruited yet another admiring fan.

Green was too driven to let jealousy override his desire to understand his competitor. "So what exactly are they doing?"

Although the consultant could not ascertain the core reasons for the cultural discrepancy, she spent the next hour simply describing various aspects of Telegraph's culture. "Apparently, there is almost no politics, very little voluntary turnover, and relatively few lawsuits brought by disgruntled employees. Even most of the former employees I spoke to raved about the firm's culture."

The executive team listened closely, asked questions, and scribbled notes like college students the day before a final exam.

The consultant eventually concluded her remarks: "Essentially they have an organization that is so sound, so"—she struggled for the right word—"so healthy that it makes them immune to most threats. This, more than anything else they're doing, seems to be driving their success financially, strategically, and competitively. I wish I knew exactly how they did it."

Vince spoke for the first time in an hour. "So do I." Standing now, he waved and forced a smile to say thank you to the consultant and left the room immediately.

No one could have known that he already had an idea.

Now where did I put that phone number?

PART TWO

The History

TWO CEOS

n many ways, Rich O'Connor and Vince Green were alike. Besides being CEOs of the area's top technical consulting firms, they were essentially likable and decent men. Both were tireless workers, fierce competitors, and committed husbands and fathers.

They also happened to receive their training at U.C. Berkeley's business school at the same time. Vince had worked with a top management consulting firm before B-school. During his two years at Berkeley, he followed the stock market religiously, maintained contact with business associates, and read as many analyst reports as he could get his hands on. He graduated near the top of his class.

Rich also earned impressive grades but maintained a relatively low profile in the process. To earn extra cash, he waited tables and tutored undergraduate students, and when he wasn't working or in class, he could be found at the psychology lab where his wife-to-be worked. Because Rich spent so much time away from the business school, he didn't establish quite as many close relationships with classmates as most others did.

When Vince decided to start his own consulting firm just a few years out of school, no one was surprised. When Rich did the same thing two months later, no one noticed.

The timing for getting into technical consulting was ideal, and for their first three years in business, both firms grew dramatically. Each CEO believed his success was the result of extremely hard work, a little luck, and amazing attention to detail within his respective firm.

Both of them received regular reports about virtually every consulting engagement that their firms took on. They knew where every dollar was being spent, how much every client owed, and which competitors were bidding on which projects.

During this time Rich and Vince developed a cordial though somewhat distant relationship. Although the two rivals respected one another, they also knew that the other would be glad to take his business away from him if he lost his edge. So they were determined to never lose their edge.

Neither firm established any discernible advantage over the other, and they shared much of the emerging local spotlight when it came to consulting. Vince liked to say that their companies maintained a degree of balance that made coexistence possible, even enjoyable.

Until something changed.

Out of nowhere, Telegraph seemed to gain an advantage over its rival. Before he knew what was happening, Vince found himself increasingly frustrated by his firm's inability to compete with Telegraph on a variety of issues. What he didn't understand at the time was that in spite of all their similarities, he and Rich O'Connor had suddenly become quite different CEOs.

DESPERATE EPIPHANY

I t happened late one night while Rich sat alone in his home office, contemplating selling his beloved three-year-old company.

He was about to break under the pressure of trying to balance his family and his successful but demanding business. It seemed that with every passing month, there was more to know—competitive analysis, technology advancements, industry trends, client updates—and less time to learn about it all. But Rich prided himself on knowing his firm inside and out, and he always found a way to stay on top of what was going on at Telegraph.

It was when he missed his third consecutive Little League game that things began to unravel. He and his wife had begun to lose patience with his increasingly unmanageable schedule, and as hard as he tried, Rich could see no relief in sight. Selling the firm and taking on a less demanding job seemed like the only way to alleviate the pressure on him and his family.

But the company had become such a part of Rich's life that he was unable to pull the trigger on a sale. So he decided to try an experiment. For three months he would quietly limit himself to fifty-hour workweeks—far below his usual seventy— which would give Rich plenty of time for his family. At the end of the experiment, if the firm were showing any signs of distress, he would sell.

For the first month he struggled, often bringing work home with him in violation of his personal pact. Trying desperately to handle the same set of responsibilities in less time, Rich only seemed to be falling further behind. Both his family and his staff were equally unhappy with the change, one that they really didn't understand.

Then, during another long and painful night in his home office, Rich made a decision that would change his career, his company, and his life forever.

On the verge of resigning himself to giving up the firm, he decided to make one final, desperate attempt at success. Instead of scouring his schedule each week in search of activities that he could eliminate, Rich decided to turn the nature of his inquiry upside down. He wrote a simple question on a piece of paper:

WHAT IS THE ONE THING I DO THAT REALLY MATTERS TO THE FIRM?

Rich stared at the question for almost an hour. Nothing came to him.

Then he suddenly began to laugh to himself. Even he wondered if the situation wasn't driving him a little crazy.

But nothing about the way Rich felt was irrational. In fact, his laugh was driven by equal parts of absurdity, simplicity, and insight. As the gravity of his breakthrough soaked in, Rich began to write his thoughts down on paper.

After almost two hours, Rich had abandoned his goal of identifying a single area of focus in his job. Instead, he expanded it to four basic activities—disciplines, really—which he neatly captured on a yellow piece of legal paper. He placed it inside his briefcase and went to bed with a sense of excitement, relief, and hope that he hadn't felt since starting the firm three years earlier.

PRACTICE

◯

When Rich woke the next morning, his sense of relief from the previous evening had faded somewhat. But when he arrived at work, he removed the yellow paper from his briefcase, stared at it for a few minutes, and felt his excitement begin to resurface almost immediately.

Taping the yellow list to the top of his desk, Rich could not stop thinking about the four disciplines that he had discovered the previous night. For the next few mornings, he began his day by reviewing the list and making necessary adjustments to his schedule. After only a week, Rich's mind set had begun to change dramatically.

Within a few more weeks, Rich found himself thinking very little about his competition, and he lost interest in many of his previous duties, like reviewing monthly billing records and expense details. He was leaving the office at 6:30 every evening, and without his usual portfolio of reports and other reading material.

More and more of Rich's responsibilities were being delegated to his staff members, who were quietly speculating that he might be preparing to let go of the business.

But soon it became clear to everyone that Rich was more engaged than he had been in almost a year. In spite of his delegation of various responsibilities, Rich's meetings took on a new sense of urgency and clarity. In fact, after just a few months, his staff saw his management style evolve toward a simpler, more focused approach.

During meetings, Rich asked more pointed questions than ever before. He resisted the temptation to dive into each and every topic, if the temptation still existed at all. Perhaps most important, and certainly most notably, he spent more time listening during staff meetings, and when he did jump into a conversation, it was usually to refocus people on the topic at hand.

Over the course of the year, Telegraph flourished and became the clear darling of the technical consulting arena.

During that time Rich guarded his schedule ferociously. Aside from occasional client visits and the unavoidable formalities required of a chief executive, everything that he did had something to do with at least one of the disciplines on "the yellow sheet," as it came to be known by a few of the Telegraph executives. They often teased Rich, accusing him of being obsessed with the list. But no one complained about it.

Interestingly, only a handful of people actually knew what was on the yellow sheet, which was odd because Rich didn't take any steps to conceal it or keep it confidential. But few people ever asked about it, and so it remained something of a mystery, which was okay with Rich because no one else really needed to understand it.

He certainly never suspected that it would become the blueprint of an employee's plan to destroy the firm.

THE GATEKEEPER

○

From the moment he began using the disciplines on his yellow sheet, Rich was continually narrowing the scope of his responsibilities to a core set of activities. One of the areas that he most adamantly insisted on being involved in, and which had a profound connection to each of the four disciplines, was the hiring of new employees.

More than a third of Rich's fifty-five-hour workweeks (fifty was just not realistic for him) was spent interviewing potential hires. Initially he insisted on seeing every candidate who cleared the first round of interviews. As the company grew, he limited himself to senior managers and partners. Even this proved to be a strain, but one that Rich gladly endured.

In addition to the time he dedicated to interviews, every other Monday morning he spent two full hours with new hires, welcoming them to the company and orienting them to the Telegraph way of life. He then spent another couple of hours with current employees, listening to their ideas and concerns.

At least once a year, Rich's guardian-like executive assistant, Karen, pleaded with him to cut back on both of these activities so he could enjoy a more manageable schedule. But he wouldn't hear of it. Other than running his weekly staff meetings, Rich felt that his involvement in hiring and orientation was one of his most important roles.

As a result of Rich's diligence and focus, the company rarely made bad hires, at least not at a senior level. His team strongly believed that this was one of the reasons Telegraph had become a great company.

But even great companies make mistakes.

ASLEEP AT THE GATE

Contrary to the beliefs of outsiders—media, competitors, even his own friends—Rich's success was not as easy to maintain as it looked. Even with his more manageable schedule, he was constantly focused on the list, and immersing himself in one or more of the four disciplines. It was a regimen he gladly accepted.

But every human being gets tired, and after eight years of running the company, Rich O'Connor had become very tired.

So, with some urging from his wife, he agreed to take a sabbatical of sorts, six weeks with his family at Lake Tahoe. No e-mail. No conference calls. The only connection to work would be a weekly fifteen-minute update from his trustworthy COO, Tom Givens.

When Tom called after just three days at the lake, Rich knew it must be important.

"Hey, I'm sorry to do this. I know we're supposed to talk on Tuesdays, but I need your go-ahead on something right away."

Rich was secretly glad to be talking to Tom. He wasn't yet comfortable with the idea of being away from the firm for so long. He joked with his colleague: "Don't apologize to me. You're going to have to deal with Laura. If she finds out I'm talking to you, you'll be looking for a new job."

Tom laughed. "Okay. I'll keep it short. I think I've finally found a replacement for Maurine, and I want to make an offer. It's the guy from Seattle who you spoke to on the phone before you left."

"But I won't be able to meet him for a few weeks still. I thought we agreed to hold off on . . ."

Tom tended to interrupt people as soon as he knew where they were headed. It was a quality that, after many earnest attempts, he was unable to correct. No one held it against him. "But, Rich, I think this is a special situation. The guy knows how to manage the HR side of acquisitions, and he has a résumé that looks better than yours and mine put together. He's got two other offers—one is from Greenwich—so we need to move right away. And Joel over at Mena Ventures says he's good."

None of this persuaded Rich. "First of all, I don't care if Greenwich or anyone else is offering him a job. And second, you know how I feel about this. Especially someone at this level. Sorry, Tom. It'll have to wait."

Rich was accustomed to fighting Tom and his other reports on issues like this from time to time. And he didn't mind doing so. In fact, there was something comforting about it. He recognized that it was Tom's job to get things done as quickly as possible, which included hiring enough employees, while it was his own responsibility to preserve the culture, which included making sure those people were a good fit for Telegraph. Everyone appreciated the balancing effect of Rich's role, even if it made for occasional episodes of constructive conflict.

Trying one last time to see if he could persuade his boss, Tom worded his plea carefully. "Rich, you know that I buy into the importance of your interviews. But this isn't the CFO position we're talking about, or even a practice director for that matter. It's the head of human resources. And we aren't going to find someone else this qualified any time soon."

Maybe it was because he was on vacation with his family, but for the first time Rich O'Connor didn't hold his ground completely. "What did everyone think of him?"

Shocked that he had an opening, Tom couldn't help but exaggerate a little. "They loved him. They couldn't believe the strength of his résumé. And with the acquisitions we've got coming early next year, they think he could be very useful."

After three months of serving as the acting head of HR, Tom was desperate to fill the position. He decided not to mention that Rita, Telegraph's legal counsel, hadn't met the candidate yet. Most important of all, he really didn't see anything wrong with the guy.

"What about the cultural stuff? I'm assuming he meets all three of the criteria." Rich didn't need to remind his COO about the importance of the firm's values. All employees who had been with Telegraph for more than a few months knew that no matter how impressive their background or skills might have been, they had made it into the firm because they were found to be humble, hungry, and smart.

Tom hesitated just a little. "I think so. Yes. He does."

Rich almost laughed. "Come on, Tom. That's no ringing endorsement. Does he or doesn't he?"

"Well, everyone who's seen him thinks he's extremely smart."

"Which is the least important of the three," Rich reminded him.

"Right. And in terms of hunger, according to his references, he has the work ethic of a mule. They practically had to send him home half the time at Jensen."

That wasn't necessarily what Rich was looking for in staff members, but it didn't hurt. "What about humility?"

Tom cleared his throat. "We *think* he's humble. We checked his references and heard nothing negative." Tom searched for more evidence to support his wishful thinking. "We did speak to one person who worked for him, someone he actually wants to bring with him at some point. She thinks the guy walks on water. And by the way, she might be able to fill that internal communication position you've been talking about."

Rich ignored Tom's persuasive maneuver. "How did he interview? Did you take him to the pier?"

Rich liked to test candidates who were on the verge of being hired by taking them places completely outside the typical interview experience, to see how they would react. Pier 39 was one of his favorites, because its touristy nature made it chaotic and tacky enough to unnerve someone who wasn't down to earth.

"We didn't," Tom admitted. "Unfortunately, we only had a few hours for all the interviews. But everyone seems to like him."

Rich didn't care if people liked the guy. He knew that most people at this level had learned how to be likable during interviews. "What did Rita think?"

Tom winced. "Rita was out of the office today, and she's been too busy to do a phone interview yet."

Rich was silent, so Tom rallied to try and save the situation. "Listen, we both knew that replacing Maurine was going to be impossible. We all want to pull her out of retirement, but we can't. And I just don't think we're going to find someone like her no matter how long we wait."

The silence on the other end of the line told Tom to keep talking: "Besides, we did most of the behavioral interview, and everyone, including Janet and Mark, agreed that we should hire him. And as soon as she can, I'll have Rita talk to him."

Yet more silence, so Tom added, "And I think you need to start trusting us on things like this."

That was the clincher. Rich would later claim that he momentarily lost his ability to separate his role as a vacationing husband and father from his responsibility for protecting the interests of the firm. Whatever the case, Tom couldn't believe it when, after a long pause, his boss said, "Okay. Have Rita meet the guy, and then if she says he's all right, do it. What's his name again?"

"Jamie. Jamie Bender. You're going to like him." The next morning, Rich felt an odd sense of relief at having relinquished a little of his responsibility to Tom. *Nothing terrible has happened,* he thought to himself. *Maybe I've been overestimating the importance of my role.*

Just three months later, Rich would be beside himself with frustration about Jamie, and he would have only himself to blame.

MISORIENTATION

◯

Because Rich still had almost a month of sabbatical remaining, Jamie Bender began his tenure at Telegraph without meeting his new CEO face-to-face. Although he had two pleasant but formal telephone conversations with Rich after accepting Tom's job offer, those were no substitute for meeting the man in person. And in addition to circumventing the formal interview process, Jamie missed out on Rich's orientation program, which would prove costly.

No one walked away from a Rich O'Connor orientation speech without a clear sense of whether they would ultimately be a fit within Telegraph. In those rare cases when misfits slipped through the rigorous interview process, within a few months they usually came to the conclusion that they didn't belong at the firm. During exit interviews, most of them indicated that their first hint of a problem came during orientation.

Tom did his best to fill in for Rich. He covered the fundamentals of the business as well as Rich could have, and even made a point of spending sufficient time talking about the firm's culture. But there was nothing quite like hearing Rich's passionate description of why he started the company and what he expected of the people who worked there.

When Rich returned from his sabbatical and finally had the chance to meet Jamie, he immediately sensed that something wasn't right. But he decided that he was being overly judgmental because he hadn't interviewed Jamie himself. *I probably wouldn't have approved of Maurine or Tom right away either if someone else had hired them,* he reasoned.

During the next few months, Rich worked closely with Jamie on a handful of projects and was surprised at what little progress he was making in terms of becoming more comfortable within the company. Jamie's work itself was adequate, though certainly not spectacular. It was his demeanor that concerned Rich the most.

While Jamie was certainly smart enough to make it at Telegraph, he didn't seem to share the hunger and humility of his colleagues. Though he worked a substantial number of hours, he seemed more concerned about himself than the good of the company. And when it came to sharing credit for any accomplishments that he was involved in, Jamie often seemed to crave individual attention.

After a few more months of the same dynamics, Rich's intuition became undeniable. He was convinced that Jamie was just not a perfect cultural fit. In fact, he wasn't close.

During staff meetings and one-on-ones, Jamie never offered strong opinions. In fact, Rich couldn't remember one instance when Jamie had challenged the opinion of a colleague, not to mention Rich himself. Some basic element of authenticity seemed to be missing.

But Tom and the other staff members saw Jamie as a symbol of Rich's trust and their good judgment, so naturally they wanted him to succeed. Whenever Rich expressed his concerns about Jamie to one of them, they usually came to the defense of their new HR executive. Even Jamie himself eventually became aware that his peers were in his corner, though he didn't yet realize how he would later be able to leverage their support.

For a while, Rich's staff was able to keep their boss at bay about Jamie. After all, Rich knew that their intentions were good. And because he genuinely wanted to trust them in this matter, he backed off.

Finally, after a few more awkward weeks, Rich decided that the time for waffling was over. *I've worked too hard to build this company* . . . Even in his mind he never seemed to finish that sentence.

HESITATION

T hough most of the CEOs he knew dreaded the ritual, Rich enjoyed doing performance reviews for his staff members. In fact, he insisted on doing them every quarter, believing that letting more than three months go by between formal feedback sessions was irresponsible. And because busy travel schedules and increasing demands on everyone's time made informal feedback harder than ever, Rich came to value these sessions more and more. Even when the news he had to deliver was not particularly good.

Such was the case with Jamie Bender.

Rich was not about to mince words with Jamie, and over the years he had learned that taking quick action in situations like this was always better than delaying the inevitable. With a performance review scheduled for that day, he decided that it provided as good a forum as any for doing what he knew was right for the company.

As he always did in cases like this, Rich went to see his legal counsel, Rita. She usually enjoyed his visits, but today her boss seemed particularly focused. "Rita, I want to let Jamie go. What do we need to do?"

Surprised by the pointed nature of the remark, Rita almost laughed. "Whoa. Where's this coming from? I thought things were improving."

"Not in my opinion. Look, we made a hiring mistake. It was my fault. I know you all thought he would be a good fit, but it's my job to press hard on this issue."

Rita looked a little surprised. "Well, I never thought he was a good fit. In fact, I told Tom that I thought Jamie seemed a bit insecure."

Rich looked surprised, then relieved, as though he had just found yet another clarifying piece of his puzzle. "Listen, I suppose I can't really blame Tom for ignoring a few warning signs. He wanted to get someone in here, and that's his job. I should have insisted on maintaining my part of the process."

Rita seemed to be waiting for Rich's next sentence, so he continued. "Anyway, I'm giving him his performance review this afternoon, and it's time for me to make things right."

Probably because she had just finished a rare and painful termination lawsuit and because she felt bad for letting Tom goad her into approving of Jamie, Rita felt the need to discourage her boss: "I'm not sure that would be such a good idea right now. If you ask me, Jamie is starting to fit in a little better. And we haven't done anything even remotely resembling a warning, verbal or otherwise."

That's exactly the problem, Rich thought. He could almost feel the Jell-O he was walking through begin to solidify as he spoke. "Come on, Rita. Don't give me that lawyer crap. He's a vice president. He signed a contract saying he could be terminated at any time. I don't care if we *are* in California."

Rita laughed. "I know. Technically, you're right. But I think a guy at this level needs a little more rope."

Rich was adamant now. "No. Less rope. Senior people should get less rope, because in the process of hanging themselves, they snag other people too."

Rita realized that there was no changing her boss's mind, so she offered him a compromise. "I'll tell you what. How about if you give him a Tom Clancy?"

Rich didn't catch on, so she explained. "A *Clear and Present Danger* review. Tell him that if you don't see improvement fast, he's going to be on his way out."

Rich considered it, then nodded as though he had no choice. He trusted Rita. "Okay. But it isn't going to be pretty."

Rita winced and wished him luck.

CONFRONTATION

B y the time Rich arrived back at his office for the meeting, Jamie was there waiting for him. Like most people who didn't understand Rich, he was always struck by the simple, unimpressive nature of his CEO's office. It diminished his boss's stature in Jamie's eyes.

Rich sat down at the wooden conference table where Jamie was seated, and began. "Jamie, this isn't going to be an easy conversation." Rich steeled himself and looked directly at his VP of HR, who seemed surprised at first, but almost immediately regained his composure.

"It's not? Why is that?"

"Because I'm not . . ." Rich hesitated, wondering if he was getting soft. "I'm not comfortable with your performance, your role." He suddenly decided to be completely up front, even if Rita might not have approved. "I'm just not sure you're a fit here."

Jamie was remarkably good at appearances. He smiled confidently, crossed his legs, and responded in a manner that was ever so slightly condescending: "It looks like we have something to talk about then."

Rich couldn't decide if Jamie's confidence was impressive or threatening. He plowed on. "I wish there was something more concrete to give you here, but I'm afraid it's about your behavior more than anything else. I'm not sure that you've developed real, honest relationships with the rest of my team, and frankly, I don't feel like I know how to connect with you. Do you know what I mean?"

Again, Jamie appeared to be unmoved by the directness of the remark. Inside he was boiling. "Well, after less than six months, I guess I'm not surprised that I haven't completely filled Maurine's shoes. That has been a challenge for me. But I have to say that I don't consider my relationship with you to be a bad one. In fact, when I think about all the CEOs I've worked for over the years, I'd say that working for you has been a pleasure."

Even Rich was not completely immune to that kind of flattery. He eased off, but just barely. "That's fine and all, Jamie, but I need you to be more open with the team. I want them to feel like you're not holding anything back. That means you need to be able to admit when you make mistakes, and call it out when they do. I just don't see you doing that."

Jamie began his response with a lie: "I understand where you're coming from completely. And I'd have to say that your points are fair." After pretending to be deep in thought for a few long seconds, Jamie sat up straight in his chair. "Let's do this, Rich. Give me three more months. I've just hired my own communication specialist, and I'm starting to feel more comfortable with my team, as well as yours." He paused, but not long enough for Rich to respond. "And the annual planning session is three weeks away. That will give me a chance to build relationships with everyone and show you who I am. We'll look back on this in a year and laugh."

Rich had expected more of a fight. Letting himself be impressed by Jamie's mature reaction, he agreed to the plan. "But I want to check in with you every couple weeks to monitor progress. And I won't lie to you, Jamie. I'm an impatient man. I might not be able to wait another three months if I don't see the right things happening."

Jamie smiled, masking both his relief and anger as much as possible. "I'll look forward to it." As he got up to leave, he stopped. "Oh, I'm assuming that the list you keep on your desk is not for public consumption."

"Well, I don't make a habit out of posting it on the Internet, but it isn't a secret, if that's what you mean."

"I was just thinking that it might be helpful for me to be on the same page as you, so to speak, especially during the next few months."

"Fine." Without even thinking, Rich began to pull back on the tape. "I don't think I've removed this in five years," he thought aloud. Just before the last piece of tape came up, the paper ripped. Rich paused for a second, as if he was deciding whether to be upset about tearing his famed yellow checklist. But he just shrugged and handed it to Jamie. "Here you go. Have Karen make a copy for you."

"Thanks." Jamie took the paper and headed for the door.

Rich couldn't quite pinpoint his own emotions. He felt a bizarre combination of regret and guilt. Regret for opening himself up to someone he wasn't comfortable with, and guilt for being suspicious in the first place. But that feeling dissipated as soon as Jamie returned the paper and left Rich's office.

Three weeks later it would return, only stronger.

THE VIRUS

○

To most people who met him, Jamie Bender seemed like a decent enough guy. But he had a few major flaws. At the top of the list was an inability to deal with confrontation. His deep fear of failure and rejection had trailed him his entire career, and as he grew older, it seemed to be gaining ground.

But Jamie was brilliant in a variety of ways. He tested off the charts in standardized tests to get into B-school. More important, he had developed a control of his emotions and a personal charm that masked his insecurities, and he had learned to leverage these skills in every way possible. In other companies where he had worked, these were enough for him to get by, even succeed. After all, in the right environment, Jamie was extremely likable. But with Rich, he could see the walls closing in fast.

Jamie knew that if this had occurred in the past, he would have put his résumé together, found a "better opportunity," and moved on. But that wasn't such an attractive option now. For one, he was actually beginning to understand and appreciate what was going on at Telegraph. On a more practical level, he had just moved his family to a new city. And even if he could leave the company, as a vice president he wouldn't be able to shake something like this from his résumé so easily. He would have to find a way to survive at Telegraph, if only for another six months, and then maybe find another job in the area.

For the first time in his career, Jamie felt trapped. And people who are trapped tend to do crazy things.

MENDING FENCES

○

I t had been almost six months since Jamie had turned down the offer to become Greenwich's vice president of human resources. He remembered that Vince Green had seemed particularly agitated by his decision to join Telegraph, even swearing about his rival at one point. And Jamie had sensed even then that he should not throw away Green's phone number. The memory of that moment gave Jamie hope.

Certainly Green would be interested in talking to Jamie. For one, the two men shared a frustration with Telegraph. More important, Jamie had information that he might find interesting.

At the time Jamie called, Green was on the verge of abandoning his almost morbid curiosity about Telegraph, and resign himself to never understanding his rival. Now Jamie was about to suck him back in.

Always the purposeful diplomat, Jamie chose his words carefully. "I know this is awkward, Vince, and I would understand if you didn't want to talk to me" (in truth he knew otherwise), "but I think that my decision to choose Telegraph over Greenwich might have been a poor one." Jamie was sure that those words would be music to Vince's ears.

"Don't be ridiculous, Jamie. It's good to hear from you. What's going on with you over there?" Green was always glad to hear about a competitor's imperfections.

"Well, I'd like to keep this between the two of us . . ."

"Of course, don't worry about it," Vince assured him a little too quickly.

"Well, things are fine, I guess. Not perfect, but I'm sure I'll manage." Jamie decided to come right to the point. "Well, I'd like to stay in touch with you, just in case I decide that this isn't the right place for me. I hope that you'd be open to talking to me again if . . ."

Green interrupted his prodigal suitor. "Listen, Jamie, I would be happy to talk to you again. Things like this happen all the time. We lose people to Telegraph; they lose people to us. Sometimes people change their minds."

Even after just six months on the job, Jamie knew that Green was exaggerating the regularity of Telegraph departures. Still, he was relieved.

Green continued. "Why don't we touch base every few months to see how you're doing?"

Jamie agreed, thanked Green for his understanding, and hung up. *How am I going to get through the annual planning session?* he wondered.

OFF-SITES

Contrary to the assumptions of his rivals, Rich O'Connor had no tolerance for touchy-feely off-site meetings. In fact, his staff had come to refer to his meetings as "hug-free zones," a term they coined during Telegraph's first management retreat five years earlier. It was then that Maurine, Jamie's predecessor, insisted on doing a team-building exercise off-site and invited a consultant to do a half-day session for the Telegraph staff.

Her consultant opened the meeting with a feeble but innocuous trust-building exercise in which the executives were blind-folded and had to solve a simple problem using only their voices and sense of touch. The consultant could not see Rich rolling his eyes behind his blindfold; if he had, he certainly would not have attempted the next exercise.

After the team had shed their blindfolds and were seated around the conference table, the consultant asked them to write their birth dates on a name tag and place it on their shirt so others could see. Maurine and everyone else in the room, with the apparent exception of the consultant, noticed that Rich's ears had suddenly turned red, a leading indicator that he was getting frustrated.

As soon as the consultant started listing everyone's astrological signs, the rest of Rich's face went red. He stood from his seat to protest, but before he could say anything, Maurine headed off the catastrophe: "Let's take a five-minute break so we can check voice mail." The room dispersed like a class of sixth-graders headed for recess.

When the executives returned, all evidence of the consultant was gone, and Maurine was standing in front of them sheepishly. "Let me just say, I had absolutely no idea! A friend of mine recommended this guy, and I guess I assumed he knew what he was doing."

Her colleagues could see how embarrassed Maurine was. Tom broke the silence with a statement he delivered in his most serious voice: "I was really worried there for a second. I thought Rich, being a Leo and all, was going to kill the guy." The room erupted in laughter.

That consultant, whose name everyone had forgotten, became something of an anonymous legend at Telegraph. In fact, every time Maurine planned an off-site, she tried to include at least one reference to a fictitious exercise that was sure to incite the humor and horror of her colleagues and their non-touchy-feely leader.

Jamie was accustomed to dealing with executives who proclaimed a distaste for all things soft. But he had found that most of them were more open to behavioral exercises than they were willing to admit. So he decided that it would be okay to push Rich and his team outside their comfort zone, if only for a few hours.

When they saw that the first item on the agenda was called "Controlled Confrontation," the management team assumed it was Jamie carrying on the same humorous tradition that Maurine had started. In fact, they thought it was a pretty clever title for Jamie's first meeting—just the sort of topic that would touch a nerve among the staff.

No one knew that Jamie was unaware of the humor.

MEADOWOOD

○

ost off-site sessions took place at a nearby hotel, which Rich and his team preferred for a few reasons: it was a short drive from San Francisco, it had a nice conference center, and perhaps most important, the hotel chain was a client of Telegraph and gave the firm a special rate. While they weren't afraid to spend money when necessary, Rich and his staff were proud of their culture of eliminating superfluous expenses.

The annual planning session was a different animal. For one, it was a two-day affair. Second, it was held at a resort called Meadowood, an understated but elegant facility in the Napa Valley, an hour's drive north of San Francisco.

For the past three weeks since his performance review with Rich, Jamie had been observing his boss and his peers more closely than ever before. As a result, two things became clearer to him. One, Telegraph had something special going. Two, Jamie was falling further and further away from being part of it. He would have to do something drastic, and soon.

As he rode in the shuttle bus through the wine country on the way to Meadowood, Jamie felt ill, and not because of the winding roads. He hadn't felt such pressure in his career since, well, maybe never.

By 11:00 A.M., everyone had arrived in the conference room and settled around the U-shaped table. Rich stood and delivered what, for him, was a customary opening talk. "I'll keep this short, because we have a lot to cover during the next two days. This meeting marks our eighth consecutive year of revenue growth, profitability, and general success at Telegraph. As always, I thank you for your effort, your passion, and your commitment. I think you know that those are not empty words." Tom could not help but crack a smile at the understated nature of his boss. Rich continued. "But let me say, as I've said before, that it is critical that we not take our success for granted. Some of the best companies in the world, with greater market share and brand equity than ours, have grown complacent and assumed that their continued success was inevitable, only to watch helplessly as it all slipped away." They had heard this message before, but Rich's sincerity never let them ignore it.

He brought the point home: "If you think about the achievements we've made over the years, you can trace their roots back to one place and one time: this annual session. So let's work hard, engage one another, and find a way to suck every bit of productivity out of the next two days. And if we can, let's have a little fun too." Rich smiled and sat down.

47

Jamie was dumbfounded. Though he would not be able to admit it until months later, for the first time in his brief stint at Telegraph, he was beginning to understand why everyone seemed to admire Rich. But Jamie wouldn't let himself go there. That would mean increasing the pain that he would ultimately feel if he failed, which was seeming more and more likely.

Rich looked over to Jamie, who was scheduled to kick off the first part of the program. "You're up first, Jamie."

Always able to portray calm and composure in the face of stress, Jamie began. "Okay, I'm going to make a change in the agenda. Instead of doing our team-building exercise at the beginning of the session, I'm going to move it to the end. I think that will work best. So that means we'll begin with Tom's overview of the strategic plan."

No one had the slightest idea that Jamie had just panicked. To them it had seemed like a simple change, so they opened their binders and dove in.

Tom led the first discussion, which focused primarily on two potential acquisition candidates: a retail-oriented consulting firm in Sausalito and a small electronic commerce outfit in Walnut Creek. There was anything but consensus in the room about the wisdom of making either deal. For ninety minutes, the seven executives debated the merits of each transaction.

Some were in favor of both, some were against both, and still others advocated only one of the deals. Jamie needed a scorecard to understand exactly who was on which side of the issue.

At one point, Tom and Rita disagreed completely about the financial feasibility of the Sausalito acquisition. Jamie was shocked by the nature of their conversation.

Tom started the exchange. "Rita, with all due respect, the legal issues you're raising aren't enough for us to back off from this deal. If we tried to avoid every potential legal problem, we probably wouldn't get out of bed in the morning."

Rita responded carefully. "Come on, Tom, you know I'm interested in the overall financial well-being of this firm as much as you are, and that I try to balance my legal responsibilities with my general management background . . ."

As usual, Tom interrupted her. "I know, Rita. You're not a typical weenie lawyer." For just a brief second, the room was tense. Until Rita laughed.

Sarcastically she responded, "Thanks, Tom. I appreciate that."

Tom was relieved by her reaction, but slightly embarrassed too. "You know what I mean. It's just that if we don't start pulling the trigger on these types of transactions, we're going to have a hard time fixing our overreliance on high-tech clients. We need a sense of urgency here."

Mark, the VP of consulting, weighed in. "The thing is, Tom, I'm not sure I can absorb responsibility for another subject matter team, and I don't know if they have the management talent to keep up with us." He paused. "Hell, I think it might be too much for you too, especially given the growth we're expecting in the first two quarters. I think you'd be overwhelmed."

Tom waited for Mark to finish the sentence this time. "Come on, Mark. You've got to have more faith in me than that." To Jamie's surprise, Tom didn't seem angry at all.

Janet, the head of marketing, added her two cents. "I agree with Mark. Tom, you're too stretched right now, and sometimes I worry that you're going to break." She let them take in the comment and then continued in a different direction. "However, we decided two years ago that our new strategy included retail and electronic commerce. And we're a little behind Greenwich in both areas. So I think that we have to find a way to get this done, even if that means Tom has to relinquish some of his responsibilities to someone else."

This time Jamie was sure that Tom would react. And he did.

"Please, please, please, someone take away some of my responsibilities," Tom joked. Everyone smiled at their raw COO. "In all seriousness though, I'm open to suggestions."

Barry, Telegraph's CFO, spoke for the first time that morning. "This is going to be harder for you than you think, Tom. Remember what happened with me last year." Heads around the table nodded.

Rich sat and listened, as he often did, clearly following the conversation but feeling no particular need to jump in just yet.

For another ten minutes the passion and intensity in the room climbed as everyone weighed in on one side or the other. Everyone, that is, but Jamie, who felt like a spectator at a tennis match who didn't know which side to root for.

Finally, Rita stood and brought the conversation to an abrupt halt. "Frankly, this is all just a bunch of speculation, and nobody really knows the right answer. But there is one thing I am absolutely certain about, and no one here can convince me otherwise." That was a more definitive statement than anyone expected from the judicious legal counsel. The room was silent. "I have to go to the bathroom. Can we take a break?"

The tension evaporated with relief. Tom suggested, "Let's take ten minutes and regroup at 12:30. I think they're going to bring lunch in for us." The executives broke for the phones and the rest rooms.

Everyone in the room seemed to be engaged and invigorated by the nature of the discussion so far, with the exception of

Jamie. Although he maintained a confident exterior, inside he felt lost among these people. In his entire career, he had never been comfortable engaging in the kind of dialogue that he had just seen. Unconsciously he felt the need to find a chink in their armor. Anything for relief.

Rita returned to the room before the others. She was about to turn on her cell phone when Jamie approached her. "I hope you weren't offended by Tom's comments."

Rita seemed a little surprised. "I wasn't offended at all. That's just Tom." She paused. "You really thought they were harsh?"

Jamie mistakenly thought Rita was second-guessing herself. In fact, what she was doing was questioning Jamie's judgment. "Yes, I did. I'm sure he meant well, but that kind of comment can cause problems if we're not careful."

Rita thought hard about what Jamie said. "I appreciate your concern, but I don't think it's a problem. If I did, I'd tell him in a New York minute."

Jamie tried to back-pedal. "Good. Because that's important. As long as you can confront him if he steps over the line, then that, well, that's important." Even Jamie thought his reply sounded inane.

At that point the others returned to the room, and Rich reconvened the meeting with his first words in almost an hour.

"Okay, everyone. We've analyzed this every way possible. Over the past two weeks we've reviewed the financials, the projections, and all the potential deal breakers. I don't think we're lacking any critical information here. It comes down to making a decision and sticking with it. Besides, the way we execute is ultimately going to determine how successful this is anyway."

Everyone nodded, but Jamie's head was bouncing up and down like a jack-in-the-box. He was desperate to find a way to get connected to these people.

Rich called the question. "So, let's decide on the Sausalito deal first. Where do we stand?" He looked at Rita.

She breathed hard. "I still think it's too risky."

Mark shook his head to vote no. "I agree with you," he said, looking at Rita.

Janet weighed in: "I say we've got to find a way."

Tom smiled. "I'm for it, but I agree that I need some help."

Barry winced. "This is tough, but I think I'll feel worse if we don't do it than if we try and fail."

Finally, everyone else having weighed in, Jamie spoke. "I'm all for it." It seemed a little hollow, if not gratuitous.

With the verbal votes in, Rich did what he usually did in these circumstances. He shared his opinion and made the final decision. "Okay. This is certainly not a slam-dunk. There are very real concerns about workload and integration, and you've done a nice job laying them out. In fact, I've changed my mind three times already this morning." His staff smiled at the subtle compliment. "However, the strategic imperative here is overwhelming. Home growing our retail practice from what we've got will take too long. Acquisition is eventually going to be necessary, and I don't think it's going to get easier next quarter, or the one after that. So let's do it."

Jamie looked at Mark and Rita to see how they would respond. Nothing.

Then Rita spoke. "Okay. We've spent a lot of time talking about this, and we don't want to take the entire planning session on it. So let's meet in my office next Tuesday to talk about due diligence, integration, and anything else we need to do to make this successful. I'll e-mail an agenda to everyone tonight."

Mark responded first. "I've got something on Tuesday morning, so let's try to do it in the afternoon. I really want to be at that meeting."

Rita nodded and made a note on her calendar.

Jamie was dumbfounded. It was as though Rita and Mark had forgotten how they had voted. He decided they must be masking their real feelings. There had to be an underlying element of resentment in this team, and Jamie decided then that the only way to take the pressure off himself was to unearth it.

THE DAY OF RECKONING

A social event was Jamie's most comfortable setting, and that night at dinner he regained some of his confidence. He made sure to spend time with Rita, rebuilding any damage he might have done during the break earlier that day. And he told a hilarious and self-deprecating HR joke during dinner, purposefully showing everyone that he could laugh at himself. Jamie was beginning to believe he could pull this off.

But by the next morning, his sense of dread returned. He knew that by the end of the day he would have to engage more, and then lead a meaningful confrontation exercise around leadership. He had an idea, but whether he could actually pull it off, he wasn't sure.

The day's session began with Rich's quarterly review of the company's overall plan, which, as far as Jamie could tell, had changed very little since the previous quarter. Still, Rich covered every bit of it, point by point. The company's underlying purpose for the business. Its behavioral values. Its business definition. Major organizational objectives. Everyone was rapt, as though they were hearing it for the first time.

The rest of the day proceeded much as the previous one had. The team hashed out many of the operational and strategic issues facing the firm—everything from marketing to partnerships to facilities. And throughout the day, skirmishes broke out among the team members, each one leading Jamie to conclude that he might never be able to do this.

One particular discussion made an impression on Jamie, not because of its fireworks, but ironically, because of the ease with which a potentially sticky decision was made. Rita announced that the firm had no luck leasing more space in the building where it currently resided. She verbalized what everyone else was thinking. "We either need to move two of our departments to another site, or find a new home for the entire company. I've identified two options for each scenario."

Tom couldn't believe they had already run out of space. He had hoped to avoid this issue for as long as possible. "I guess this is a good problem to have, although it scares the hell out of me. How far away would the satellite office be?"

Rita looked at her notes. "Three blocks. And it has room for forty-five employees."

Mark didn't want to move his department. "I've got almost that many now, so it looks like a no-go for me. What about you, Janet?"

"Well, I'll have twenty by the end of the year, so I could probably make that work for a year or two."

Rich decided to guide the conversation. "It sounds like everyone is leaning toward the satellite option rather than moving the entire firm." They could tell he was trying to make a statement of some kind, and Rita took his bait. "The idea of moving the entire company is pretty awful to me. The last move took so much time we lost almost three weeks with all the hassles." She was always the practical one.

Rich was not. "We can dive into the short-term pros and cons of these options, but I think it would be better to step back and ask ourselves what would be in the best long-term interest of who we are."

Mark seemed puzzled, so Rich explained. "Think about our strategy and our history."

Tom caught on right away. "Yeah, we're always talking about the importance of cross-functional teams and tearing down silos. Having two sites is not going to help that."

Rich added, "And if we're going to absorb the new retail team, we'll want to have them mixed in with everyone, not just Janet's people. Otherwise they'll never really blend."

Mark came around. "That's true, because if we don't give them a ton of support right away, I'll never hit the $3 million retail number."

As valid as these points were, the practical implications were still daunting for Rita. "But next quarter we're going to open a Seattle office. We have to get used to multiple sites eventually, don't we?"

"Yes, but whenever we can avoid it . . ." Rich interrupted his own thought. "Look, I think location is vital when it comes to people communicating and working together. Two blocks away or two hundred miles—it's pretty much the same."

Tom pitched in. "Remember what it was like working with Trinity Systems last year? Three buildings on the same campus, and we had one hell of a time getting strategic planning and marketing to communicate. It was ridiculous."

"You're right. I know it." Rita relented. "But my life is going to be a mess."

"What are the two options for new space?" Tom wanted to keep the conversation going.

Rita exhaled. "Well, there's a nice building with plenty of space near the new ballpark. And then there's a gorgeous space that just opened up north of the Embarcadero. It looks like a palace, but the price is pretty much the same as our other option."

Mark had a soft spot for luxury. "I vote for the Embarcadero."

This time Tom played Rich's role in the discussion. "What makes the most sense in terms of who we are?"

Rita had an answer right away. "The ballpark. It's nice but not overly so. It's more convenient to the airport and freeways. That means shorter time for clients to get to us and for us to get to them."

Rich reminded them of their roots. "And I don't think we want our clients wondering how we can afford to live in a palace. It doesn't really fit with our commitment to humility and customer intimacy."

Rita scribbled notes on her pad. "The ballpark looks like the right answer. I'll meet with the real estate guy and see how fast we can make this happen." She turned to Barry. "Can I hire a contractor to handle this move so I don't drown here? This is a busy quarter for me."

Barry nodded. "I'll check the budget. It should be fine."

Suddenly the conversation was over. The subtlety of what had just happened almost made Jamie miss its significance. He remembered many similar conversations taking place in his career. The difference was the time frame. It had taken Telegraph less than twenty-five minutes to make a decision that other companies spent weeks, sometimes months, discussing. Making a location move usually brought out a host of sensitive issues and posturing on the part of executives. They wanted to see all the plans, argue for space, and have a guided tour. Not Telegraph. *What is going on here?* Jamie asked himself.

Rich refocused the meeting. "Okay. Before we let Jamie do the team-building exercise, let's talk about the cascading communication plan." Rich went to the flip chart at the front of the room and asked, "What are the key messages we need to bring back to our people when we get back to the office next week?"

Jamie watched as the group tossed out key issues and decisions that were made: the Sausalito acquisition, next quarter's goals, two promotions, a key change in expense policy, a new training program, and the facilities move. After fifteen minutes of discussion, they agreed to communicate everything on the list with the exception of the potential Sausalito acquisition, because it was still pending. Then they spent a few minutes talking about the right way to articulate a few of the more sensitive issues so employees had the complete picture.

As he always did at the end of a cascading session, Rich reminded them of their responsibility. "So let's all take these messages back to our staffs by the end of day Monday." He added, "And remember, if we don't do it right away, we'll forget some of the essence of the issues, and your people are going to hear about them from someone else. Don't let that happen."

Heads nodded as if to say, "Okay, okay," and everyone busily copied the material from the flip chart.

Rich then spoke the words that Jamie had dreaded. "Alright Jamie, you're up."

360° FEEDBACK

After contributing so little during the previous two days, Jamie decided that he would have to go through with his riskiest approach. The only way to save himself would be to create a major distraction, maybe even a potential crisis that he could then help to avoid. And it would have to involve Rich.

As he stood to announce the exercise, Jamie knew that there was no turning back, so there was no sense in being nervous. With all the confidence of a seven-year veteran of Telegraph, he began: "Thanks, Rich. What we're going to do today is review the results of the 360-degree feedback questionnaires that we filled out a few weeks ago. But rather than going through the feedback we received from our direct reports, we'll just focus on one another's peer input."

No one seemed to object, which wouldn't have mattered to Jamie anyway, not at this point. Still, he was relieved that they seemed to be on board.

"What we'll do is this. Everyone will be reading someone else's feedback summary. That way, we'll all get a chance to hear our own issues objectively." He handed a summary report to each member. "After each summary has been read, the person who is being reviewed can ask questions, and we can discuss the results." Everyone nodded, indicating their approval. Jamie knew that the absence of a formal, contrived program would help the team accept the exercise.

"We'll start with Tom. Who has Tom's report?"

Rich raised his hand.

Jamie gave his final instructions. "We don't have much time, so let's dive in."

Without hesitation, Rich opened the report, cleared his throat, and began reading. Tom was almost eager to hear something negative, which would provide fodder for his self-effacing humor. But virtually the entire summary was positive. When Rich finished, Tom was almost disappointed.

More than one of his colleagues found the report odd, given that they had provided at least a few morsels of constructive criticism. The only thing that was remotely constructive was Tom's tendency to interrupt people, which he gladly demonstrated the first chance he got, just for comic relief.

One by one the other executives read the summaries for their colleagues. Discussion was lively but relatively painless, because most of the feedback was positive. Any initial suspicions that they had about the accuracy of the data were overwhelmed by the supportive, complimentary nature of the comments they received. The meeting had turned into a veritable love fest.

Rich too had wondered about the relative absence of constructive feedback. But given Jamie's eroding situation and the success of the past two days, he decided that to address the issue would be an unnecessary distraction. Another time would be more appropriate. So he decided to sit back and enjoy heaping well-deserved praise on his staff members.

Only two people had yet to be reviewed: Jamie, and Rich, who would go last.

Tom would be reading Jamie's data, and before he began, the room seemed to tense up a bit. Jamie too seemed nervous, but in a likable kind of way. In fact, he was working the audience for any amount of preemptive sympathy he could get.

Mark tried to break the tension with a quick question, one that he genuinely was curious about. "Excuse me, Tom. Before you start, I'd like to know how this data was analyzed. I'm just curious about the process." Mark was careful to word the question in a way that did not sound like an attack on Jamie.

Jamie stuttered for just a moment. "Well, the data is computer tabulated, of course. And then Sophia, my new communication specialist, goes through it to identify trends and consistent themes. She's done plenty of these before."

Rita wrote something down on a pad of paper.

Mark smiled. "Thanks, Jamie. Go ahead, Tom."

Tom began. "There are three primary pieces of feedback that were evident in Jamie's data. First, it says here that everyone acknowledges the level of experience and expertise you bring to the team. Second, you put a lot of time and effort into your work." Jamie was trying to seem pleasantly surprised by the feedback. "And third, more than one of us mentioned that you could probably voice your opinions more often."

An awkward pause followed Tom's last sentence. Jamie knew when to step in. "I'd like to discuss that last point with you, if I could."

Everyone nodded enthusiastically.

Jamie took the floor. He spent the next fifteen minutes talking about how impressed he was by the quality of his colleagues, including Rich. Deftly walking the line between praise and gratuitousness, he explained how he felt humbled by their years of experience in the industry and his relative lack of involvement in Telegraph's history.

Finally, Jamie assured them that he was working hard to "cultivate a full appreciation of the culture" and that he would soon begin to "take more risks with his opinions, and push his colleagues out of their comfort zones." He certainly had learned to mirror the vocabulary of his peers, if not their attitude.

By the time he had finished, Jamie's colleagues felt compelled to offer him encouragement instead of constructive input. They served up hollow phrases, like "Give yourself a little time" and "We all have the advantage of knowing one another."

Rich thought his team had gone a little soft, but again, didn't want to create any waves so close to the end of what was generally a very positive meeting.

Finally, when the discussion had run its course and Jamie felt sufficiently propped up, he turned to Rich. Looking at his watch, "Well, we have fifteen minutes. I'll be reading Rich's review."

Jamie took out a pair of reading glasses and looked down at the page in front of him. "All right, it says here that there are four major themes in Rich's feedback." He paused for a moment, as though he was scanning the content of the page, before he began.

"Okay, it says that Rich is extremely committed to the firm and works hard for what he believes is right." Jamie paused to let his boss take in the praise. "It also says that he knows the business extremely well." Tom nodded, both to corroborate the message and to support Jamie.

Suddenly Jamie frowned, as if to distance himself from what he was about to read. "But, according to the data, he needs to trust the judgment of his staff a lot more. And be less dogmatic."

Silence.

The stark contrast between Rich's abrupt summary and that of the others was obvious to everyone in the room. Although the volume of constructive comments in Rich's review was not necessarily surprising, it seemed harsh relative to that of his peers.

Rich could not decide whether to be hurt, or angry. And if anger were his choice, who would be the target? He chose neither.

After all, he was not afraid of receiving tough feedback from his people. He genuinely welcomed their input. Over the years, they had developed a strong team precisely by creating an atmosphere of frank, naked feedback. How could he feel wronged by this relatively innocuous piece of information? But he could not deny that he did.

Jamie, who seemed genuinely concerned about the awkward situation that his boss was in, broke the silence. He demonstrated a confidence that surprised everyone. "Okay. It looks like there are a few things to talk about here. Who wants to start?"

After yet another awkward pause, Tom felt the need to salvage the situation, for both Rich's and Jamie's sakes. "As usual, I'll go first." There was nervous laughter in the room, something extremely rare for the group. "I'm not sure what everyone else was thinking, but I suppose, Rich, that you could give us the benefit of the doubt a little more often. Although I have to say that I don't really see this as a problem. And I'm not just kissing your behind."

The welcomed moment of genuine laughter quickly dissipated.

Rita chimed in. "I don't want to speak for everyone else, but I might have written something in my feedback about you having strong opinions."

Jamie could now see the possibility of relief, and he couldn't help himself. He drove the wedge in a little further. "Come on now, folks. This information comes from all of you, so let's not pretend we don't own it."

Janet hadn't spoken yet, and she didn't want to seem as if she was holding anything back. "Well, I'm not sure I wrote this in the questionnaire, but I do think you could have let Mark and me figure out the billing problems last quarter instead of having Tom step in. Every once in a while I wonder if you think we've got our clients under control."

Mark nodded, though without much enthusiasm.

Rich took in their comments with his usual thoughtfulness, but inside he felt as if something very bad had just happened. And he didn't know how to deal with it because any suspicious or defensive reaction on his part would only serve to corroborate the reports. So, as painful as it was to do so, he remained silent.

Jamie now stepped in. "Listen, folks, I'm afraid we're out of time, and the shuttle back to the office is going to be leaving in ten minutes. But let's be sure to pick this up again sometime early next week. We don't want to let it go without resolution."

Again, he seemed genuinely concerned about the unfortunate timing. No one could have known that deep inside, he was happier than he had been since joining the firm.

UNRAVELING

⬭

As hard as they tried, the team was not able to schedule a follow-up meeting to continue the discussion of Rich's 360-degree feedback. Every time someone proposed a time, at least one person on the staff had a scheduling conflict. Usually it was Jamie.

As each day went by, the momentum around having the meeting faded. Unfortunately, the bizarre dynamic that had developed during those last fifteen minutes in Napa did not. In fact, over the course of the next month, it began to take on a life of its own.

For the first time in his entire career, Rich was feeling just a little uncomfortable when he ran into his colleagues in the halls. Although barely perceptible, it was undeniable to his staff that Rich had lost some level of confidence. Although he would never sulk, his words and actions seemed more forced than they had been in almost five years. The impact of this subtle change manifested itself in troubling ways.

For one, decisions seemed to be taking longer during weekly meetings. Even the frequency of communication from Rich to employees began to fade somewhat, and it lost much of its crispness as Jamie's new communication specialist took on more of the responsibilities for deciding when and how much information to disseminate.

And there were other subtle but unsettling signs of change. Telegraph's stringent hiring process began to lose some of its teeth as Jamie made "adjustments," as he called them, always based on a legal issue of some sort. Rita, beaten down by occasional lawsuits, tended to back Jamie on these matters, giving him just the momentum he needed.

With the confidence that came with his new-found job security, Jamie even managed to chip away at a small part of the firm's performance management system, reducing some of the autonomy that managers had in rewarding employees with performance bonuses, and decreasing the frequency of mandatory reviews. He advocated these changes in the name of "greater management flexibility."

Of course, none of this would have been possible under normal circumstances. But the incremental nature of the changes, combined with Rich's slightly damaged confidence, kept the group from realizing what was happening and stopping it.

It wasn't until more than two months after the annual off-site meeting, when Rita and Mark met with Rich to discuss the final details of the Walnut Creek acquisition, that the severity of the situation hit home with the Telegraph executive team.

During that meeting, Rich did something that they had never seen: he backed off on a major strategic decision. "Mark, why don't you do a little more analysis before making any commitments to these people." He stood to leave the meeting. "You guys can make the decision without me. Just let me know what you decide."

After the meeting, Rita and Mark agreed that it was spooky to see their boss being unsure of himself, even weak. They decided they wanted to do something about it, but they didn't know what.

The next week, two things happened that proved to be the wake-up call Telegraph needed.

COLD WATER

◯

Staff meetings since the off-site session had become less and less crisp. Although Rich had begun to restore some of his outwardly positive disposition, the group knew that his passion and enthusiasm were not what they had come to expect. Still, decisions were being made, and work was getting done.

At the end of one of those meetings, Janet stood to make a statement. "Before we break, I have two pieces of news to give you, neither of which is good." She had everyone's attention. "First, Mark and I just learned that we might be losing Trinity as a client."

Tom's face went white. "What? I thought that Amy and her team had that under control."

Mark explained. "So did I. And so did Amy. She spoke to Andrew O'Brien, who said they're just not sure they're getting the same value from the relationship anymore. I guess one of their people told Amy that they've been disappointed that they haven't seen any of our senior people lately."

Rich shook his head. "Janet, let's have a meeting tomorrow to figure out a plan to fix this. You and Tom and I should all be there. We can call Andrew and straighten this out."

Janet looked down. "Well, that brings me to the next thing I want to say." She looked up at the group, and there were tears in her eyes. "I'm going to be leaving the firm."

No one spoke.

Finally, Janet explained. "Listen, you all know that Ron and I are moving out to Half Moon Bay, and I've decided to change the direction of my career. I'm going to work from home, start my own small business consulting practice, and see what I can do." She paused to regain her composure. "It's been a wonderful four years here, but I think it's a good time to move on." She sat down.

Jamie, who seemed unaffected by the announcements, excused himself. "I'm sorry. But I've got a benefits meeting to get to. I'll talk to you about exit plans later, Janet."

She nodded to him as he left.

Rita looked as though she were about to explode. She gathered her things quickly and, without looking at anyone, left the room.

Tom and Rich exchanged glances.

MOMENT OF TRUTH

W ithin twelve hours, there was an e-mail message from Rita in every executive's in-box calling a dinner meeting at a nearby restaurant in North Beach for the following Friday evening. She indicated that the subject of the meeting would be resolving Rich's 360-degree feedback discussion. She also announced that she had already checked with everyone's assistants to make sure they were free. "I'll look forward to seeing you all there," the note closed.

After seeing Rita's expression as she left the staff meeting, no one dared complain.

Three months earlier, it would have been ludicrous to think that the Telegraph executive team was dreading a meeting to discuss a difficult topic. But now it was a reality. And no one was dreading the experience more than Rich.

Not one to shirk responsibilities or avoid unpleasantness, the CEO arrived fifteen minutes early. He found the small, private banquet room at La Felce and sat at the long table by himself. In his hands he held the faded yellow list that had been taped to his desk for the past five years. He had removed it and brought it with him in the hope that it might provide some level of guidance. Though he had vowed to hide his demeanor from his people, Rich felt defeated.

The next ten minutes ticked by one second at a time. Finally, Tom, Rita, and Mark shuffled in, followed within minutes by Barry and Janet, who had another three weeks before her departure.

Tom spoke first. "Okay, let's get started."

"Where's Jamie?" Though he had asked the question, Rich seemed slightly disinterested in the answer, lost in his own thoughts.

That's probably why he didn't hear Rita when she said, "He's packing his office."

Rich frowned, as though he didn't speak Rita's language. "Excuse me?"

Rita clarified, matter-of-factly. "He's leaving the firm."

Suddenly her words registered with Rich. "What?"

77

"That's right. We decided it was time for him to go."

Rich interrupted. "You *fired* him?"

"Well, not exactly," she explained. "We went in to confront him this afternoon, but before we mentioned anything about him leaving, he resigned."

Rich could see that she was relieved. But he was confused. "Just like that?" He thought it over for a second, and then asked the obvious question. "Don't you think you should tell me about something like that?"

"We *are* telling you."

Rich was a little annoyed. "I mean beforehand."

Tom jumped in. "Come on, Rich. Ever since the Napa off-site, everything's been so bizarre. You haven't been yourself these last two months. So last week Rita and I decided that we had to deal with all of this right away." He paused. "And we did something that we're not too proud of."

Rich looked confused, and concerned.

Rita explained. "We went to Sophia, Jamie's communication specialist, and made her show us the raw data from the 360 feedback."

Rich winced at the idea of breaching the anonymity of the data.

"Believe us on this one," Tom defended. "It was the right thing to do."

Rita continued. "Get this. The words *trust* and *dogmatic* were mentioned in your entire feedback report only once. Once," she repeated, holding up her index finger.

Not having thought about the specific nature of the 360 summary report for almost two months, Rich seemed a little confused. Everyone else was smiling. They had obviously discussed all of this before.

"What's so funny?" their boss asked.

Rita blurted out: "*You* were the one who mentioned it!" She could see that he needed a little more clarification. "Here is what you wrote about yourself." She looked down at her notes and read aloud. "'Sometimes I wonder if I trust them enough. Am I too dogmatic?'" Rita laughed. "None of us wrote anything like that!"

Weeks of stress dissipated in laughter as the team realized the ridiculousness of the circumstances. As everyone settled down, the gravity of the dysfunctional situation hit them.

"So what exactly did he say?" Rich wanted to know.

"Who? Jamie?" Rita asked.

Rich nodded, and Tom jumped in before Rita could respond. "I've never seen anything like it. He basically told us that he didn't think he was a good cultural fit here. And you know what? I think he actually meant it."

Rita agreed. "Then he shook my hand and Tom's, and he asked us to apologize to you." She paused. "That's pretty much it."

Rich took it all in, still digesting the entirety of the situation, until something crossed his mind. "Wait a second. How come you guys didn't speak up during that hellish conversation in Napa? Why did you let me go through all that?"

Janet explained. "Think about it from our perspectives, Rich. We were as shocked as you were, but I assumed that maybe I was the only one who wasn't pissed at you." They laughed a little.

Mark chimed in. "Same here. How could we know for sure? And it wasn't like he made up the data. He just used the parts that you wrote about yourself, which made it that much more credible."

Tom confessed, "And I have to admit that I didn't want to put Jamie on the spot, especially in front of you. We all wanted to find a way to help the poor bastard succeed. I certainly wasn't comfortable accusing him of tweaking the data."

Rita teased Tom. "Come on, you just didn't want to have to do the HR job again."

He laughed. "Anyway, the way I see it, this is largely your fault." He was looking at Rich, who seemed confused. "You should have insisted on interviewing the guy." Tom smiled, and then added, "And I'm only half joking."

Rich nodded.

Mark asked a question that everyone was thinking. "So what's a guy like Jamie going to do now?"

Rita rolled her eyes. "Oh, I'm sure a guy like that has a backup plan."

Little did they know.

PART THREE

Green's Opportunity

REACQUAINTANCE

○

Jamie had an amazing ability to compartmentalize his thoughts, and within hours of leaving Telegraph he set his mind on getting his career back on track. He had survived the better part of a year with Rich O'Connor, and he was determined to take advantage of that fact in some way. His first call was to Vince Green.

Jamie believed he had a receptive target, and so the message he left on Vince's voice mail was to the point: "I've left Telegraph and would like to revisit the possibility of working with you at Greenwich. I'm looking forward to speaking with you." He left his home phone number.

When he first received Jamie's message, Vince didn't plan on responding at all. But three days later, when the organization development consultant ended her presentation about Telegraph's culture, Vince's interest in Jamie Bender was suddenly revived. *Now where did I put that phone number?*

After calling and making arrangements to meet Jamie the next morning, Vince decided not to get his hopes too high about what he would learn. Part of him felt guilty about talking to Jamie, so he vowed that he would toss him out of his office if he mentioned anything that remotely resembled a trade secret or intellectual property. He hoped that his desperation would allow him to keep that vow.

Vince arrived at his office in a positive frame of mind. But as he waited the thirty minutes before Jamie arrived, he found himself losing patience and self-respect.

Vince reflected on the past five years and his growing frustration as a leader. He thought hard, as he had done many times before, about why his firm lagged Telegraph and what had kept him from overtaking his rival.

It certainly isn't intelligence, he thought to himself. Few people matched Vince's intellect and analytical abilities when it came to business and consulting in particular. *And it can't be my work ethic.* Vince worked brutally long hours. A few years earlier he had heard rumors about Rich O'Connor's new "manageable schedule" and decided that it would be just a matter of time before Telegraph paid the price for its leader's softness.

When that didn't happen, Vince rededicated himself to an even more rigorous schedule, which only intensified his frustration, as well as his disdain for Rich O'Connor.

As the time of the meeting with Jamie approached, Vince became even more desperate to find the answer that he had been searching for. He entertained a hopefully absurd notion that if he could only solve this puzzle before Jamie arrived, he could cancel the meeting and preserve a modicum of dignity.

And then the intercom sounded. "Vince, your nine o'clock appointment is here."

CONTACT

Jamie had always envisioned meeting Green at a small hotel or obscure restaurant, but now that he had left Telegraph, he had no problem going directly to the Greenwich offices. In fact, it was something of a relief to be out in the open.

When Jamie arrived for the meeting, he half expected Green to be waiting at the front door of the building. He went upstairs and announced his arrival to the receptionist, and sat down to read the *Wall Street Journal* as he waited.

Spotting Jamie from across the room, Vince noticed immediately that he seemed to have aged since he had seen him just a year earlier. *That place must have worked the guy over,* he thought.

"Hello, Jamie." Vince interrupted Jamie's reading.

With a level of confidence that Vince had not remembered, Jamie returned his greeting. "Well, hello there, Vince. It's good to see you again."

Vince invited Jamie into his stylish office and motioned for him to sit in one of the leather chairs that afforded a view of Alcatraz and Angel Island.

Jamie couldn't help but marvel at the difference between the two executive offices, and Green seemed to know what he was thinking. "Yes, I've heard all about the austerity of O'Connor's office. If I hear one more thing about how frugal they are over there . . ."

Jamie joked, "I'll make sure to leave that part out."

Green laughed and searched for something to say. "Right. Well, it's good to see you again, Jamie, although I have to tell you I was pretty disappointed last year when you turned down our offer."

Jamie smiled sheepishly. "What can I say? We all make mistakes."

Green was an easier target for Jamie's wiles than Rich. "Lessons learned." Even Vince thought his response sounded like a ridiculous cliché.

Jamie broke the ice. "So, how is your VP of HR working out? Is there a chance that I might be helpful around here?" He had done enough research to know the answer to that question. Vince and his staff were looking to make a change.

"Listen, we're always looking for good people. But I would be surprised if you were legally free to come to work here for a while."

Jamie smiled. "Nope. Telegraph placed no restrictions on my ability to work with a competitor."

Vince was surprised. "Well, that's good news." He felt that the moment was now right to set the moral stage for the discussion that was about to take place. "But of course you know that if you did join us, I would insist that you not bring any proprietary information about Telegraph with you. And that goes for today's meeting too."

Jamie reacted with feigned astonishment. "Absolutely. I am a fanatic about ethical details."

Vince thought his response was a little too strong. But with the moral and legal dances out of the way, he was dying to dive in. "So, what exactly happened over there, anyway?"

Jamie took a deep breath and smiled. He had rehearsed this line: "That is one bizarre company, let me tell you."

90

Vince felt the need to begin the conversation with intellectual integrity, and so he challenged Jamie. "Well, they must be doing something right." Even he couldn't believe that he was defending Telegraph, but he would not let his need for consolation overwhelm his desire to know the truth.

Jamie knew how to spot a man's anguish, and so he offered his potential boss a bone. "Yes, they are, but that's the thing. I've looked beneath the covers, and there isn't much to see. They're not doing anything that you couldn't do tomorrow." Jamie decided to exaggerate a little to keep Vince on the hook. It worked.

"What do you mean? And again, I'm assuming you're not talking about confidential . . ."

Shaking his head, Jamie responded before Vince could finish the sentence. "No, nothing like that. It's really very simple. Embarrassingly so, if you ask me."

Vince was ready to burst with curiosity, but he tried hard to conceal his desperation. With a sense of detached interest, he pursued the issue. "Really? Tell me about that."

"Well, it all has to do with a yellow sheet of paper that Rich O'Connor keeps on his desk. It's really just a checklist of sorts, a few concepts that he calls his four disciplines. And from what

I could tell, the man is obsessed with them. He uses those disciplines to run his life." Jamie seemed to be mocking and admiring his former boss all at once.

"A checklist?" Vince was intrigued, and suddenly lost any sense of subtlety that he had tried to maintain before. "What's on it?"

Jamie decided to play with the desperate executive for just a minute. "Well, very few people actually know much about it." Immediately he could see Vince begin to panic at the thought that Jamie did not know the contents of the list. Not wanting to alienate a future employer, he let him off the hook. "But I do."

DISCIPLINE ONE

○

Jamie had decided that he would not just recite the list of disciplines for his suitor. That would diminish the fun. Instead, he would describe the unusual behaviors of Rich and his staff, and let Vince look for the thread or theme.

He all but announced this to Vince, who reluctantly agreed, and then buzzed his assistant: "Tracy, please clear my morning. . . . That's right, until after lunch. . . . Thanks." He hung up the phone. "Let's get started."

Jamie sat forward in his chair and seemed genuinely excited to be sharing all of this with Vince. "You would not believe the way these people act during meetings. I've never seen anything like it, and I've worked at a lot of different places."

Vince cracked a smile. "What do they do?" He was quietly relieved to know that someone, anyone, thought that Telegraph was weird.

"They argue constantly."

Vince was surprised. "Really?"

It was a rhetorical statement more than a question, but Jamie answered it anyway: "Oh, yeah, they don't miss any opportunities to argue. Their meetings are like internal family feuds. Someone is always getting upset about something, and people yell and shout. It reminded me of some cousins of mine. Irish and Italians."

Vince thought about his own staff meetings and wondered aloud, "I bet they're not boring at least."

Jamie laughed. "No, *boring* isn't a word I'd use to describe Rich's meetings." He noticed that just using Rich's name made Vince shrink a little.

"How do they get anything done?" Before Jamie could respond, Vince added, "And how do they avoid killing each other?"

"That's the crazy part. These people argue like brothers and sisters, but then they seem to forget about the arguments ten minutes later, just like my cousins. One of them would have a bloody nose, and the next thing you know they're laughing."

Vince was stunned. Jamie quickly clarified. "I was talking

about my cousins. I never saw anyone at Telegraph punch someone in the nose."

Vince smiled.

"Although I did think that Rita was going to cold-cock Tom a few times."

"Really?"

"Well, not exactly. But she used to get upset at him on a fairly regular basis. She actually called him an ass one night during a long meeting."

"Tom is the COO, right?"

Jamie nodded. "And Rita is the legal counsel."

Vince knew that. "Right. So the two of them didn't get along so well. That could be pretty difficult, given their respective . . ."

Jamie interrupted. "No, I never said they didn't get along. In fact, they worked very closely together. They just always seemed to fight during meetings."

"About what?"

"Budgets. Clients. Employees. You name it."

"Petty stuff?"

Jamie had to think for a second. "No, they didn't spend much time on petty topics during meetings. Usually it was something fairly important."

Vince was confused. "So how did they make decisions? The loudest one wins?"

Jamie laughed. "No, because Tom would have won them all. What they would do is argue for a while, and then someone, often Rich, would make everyone step back from the issue and cast a vote."

"So they voted on everything?"

"No, not really. Ultimately Rich would make decisions when there was no clear answer. But usually they came to a fairly quick consensus. Somehow the arguing seemed more like fact finding than advocacy. It was strange."

Vince could see that beneath all of his disparagement, Jamie admired his former colleagues. This only frustrated Vince and made him impatient.

"So what exactly is the first discipline?"

"I haven't finished describing . . ."

This time Vince interrupted. "Listen, just tell me what the first discipline is, and then you can describe it all you want."

Vince had a way of demanding something that made a person not want to test him. Jamie smiled to conceal his momentary fear, and then relented.

"Build and maintain a cohesive leadership team."

"Excuse me?"

"That's the first discipline: 'Build and maintain a cohesive leadership team.'"

Vince thought about it for a moment. "That's it?" He seemed suddenly confident and judgmental.

"Well, that's the way Rich describes it. But there is a lot more to it than that."

Vince took a deep breath and reminded himself what he was after. "Like what?"

"Well, they did something called the Myers-Briggs. You've probably heard of it."

Vince nodded. "Yeah, I think I did something like that in graduate school. I don't remember exactly."

Jamie was suddenly animated again. "Well, it's actually pretty interesting. You take a twenty-minute test and then get a report back that tells you how you make decisions and organize things."

Vince was frowning. "Sounds pretty squishy to me."

"Well, it can be. But over there, they use it to understand each other. Everyone knows everyone else's Myers-Briggs type, and they refer to it all the time."

"And that's good because . . ." Vince let Jamie finish the sentence for him.

"Well, for one it helps them avoid making judgments about each other. And it gives them a vocabulary for pointing out each other's flaws. They used to give Tom a hard time for being such an extrovert and Rita for being a 'J,' which is basically the Myers-Briggs way of saying she was anal retentive."

Now Vince was totally lost.

Jamie explained. "See, when Rich thought about making his team cohesive, he wanted them to know one another well enough so that they didn't hold anything back. Those people really do act like brothers and sisters, and when a difficult issue has to be discussed, no one hesitates. Not for a minute."

Vince turned sarcastic. "So these people were perfect, basically."

"Not at all. I think some of them are peculiar. But one thing I have to say about them is that not once did I ever hear them say anything negative about a member of the team."

"Oh, come on." Vince was incredulous.

"You didn't let me finish. I said I never heard them say anything negative that they wouldn't say directly to the person."

Vince nodded as if to say, *Oh, I get it.* It all seemed to be sinking in now.

Jamie continued. "As unusual as they were, those people cared about one another. And I suppose that if you liked them, that would be okay. For me, it was too much." Jamie didn't seem to believe the last part of his own statement.

For the first time Vince saw a clear picture of Jamie's insecurity. He actually felt bad for him, and decided to help him move on. "So, what's the second discipline, Jamie?"

DISCIPLINE TWO

J amie stood and walked over to an oak cabinet that hung on the wall near Vince's desk. He opened it and, as he expected, found a white board covered with text and graphs. "Can I erase this?"

Vince looked over the contents on the board. "Yeah, go ahead."

After neatly and methodically erasing the entire board, Jamie wrote the first discipline:

DISCIPLINE ONE: BUILD AND MAINTAIN A COHESIVE LEADERSHIP TEAM.

Unfortunately for Vince, Jamie set down his pen before writing the second one.

Jamie walked to the window and stared out toward the Bay, as though he were looking for discipline two somewhere in the tide. "The second discipline seems extremely common, but the way they go about it is anything but."

"Are you going to make me guess this one?" Vince asked dryly.

Jamie thought about it. "No, it would be too hard to explain that way." He returned to the white board and wrote the words:

DISCIPLINE TWO: CREATE ORGANIZATIONAL CLARITY.

Vince was disappointed. "There must be more to it."

Jamie half smiled. "Yes, there is. Essentially it's about eliminating confusion within the company, especially at the executive level."

"What kind of confusion?"

"Important things, like the company's identity, direction, strategy, objectives, roles and responsibilities."

"You're right. It sounds common. I don't know a single company that doesn't do this."

Jamie nodded. "I agree. Sometimes it seemed that they thought they were more clever than they really are. Do they think their competitors don't know these things?"

Jamie's rhetorical question made Vince stop and think. "How well did Rich's executive team know them?"

"Oh, they knew them. And they talked about them all the time."

"How so?"

"If they had a difficult time making a decision, they'd refer to their values, or their mission, or their strategy."

"Did they have this stuff plastered all over the place?"

Jamie rolled his eyes. "No, I tried to get them to make a poster, but Rich refused. His people just knew this stuff inside and out. I tell you, they were like a cult."

Vince didn't think that sounded so bad. *How many of my executives could recite our strategy, our objectives, our values?* he thought. *Do we even have values?*

Jamie went to the board and wrote a list next to the second discipline:

IDENTITY, VALUES, MISSION, MAJOR GOALS, OBJECTIVES, ROLES AND RESPONSIBILITIES

"I think that's it," Jamie said. "In any case, I don't think it's such a big deal."

Vince did. He copied what Jamie had written onto a legal pad, then asked, "What exactly do they mean by identity?"

Jamie responded without really thinking. "Well, their identity is all about . . ."

Vince interrupted. "Wait. I don't want to know any of their information. That's their business."

Jamie seemed genuinely embarrassed about having almost shared confidential information, even if that information was not terribly sensitive. He changed course. "Identity is about the company's hiring values and its underlying motivation."

Vince nodded. "Like core purpose and core values from *Built to Last*." He pointed to a copy of the book on his shelf. "So they actually pay attention to that stuff?"

"Yes they do. But I think too much. After a while it got old."

That's the point, Vince thought. "How did they use the values?"

Jamie rolled his eyes again. "How didn't they? They talked about those values all the time. But the place where it seemed most critical was in hiring. They were fanatics."

"Go on."

"Well, first of all, Rich insisted on being involved in the hiring of all senior people. He was considered the cultural filter, and virtually the only thing he looked for in a candidate was cultural fit."

"How exactly did he do that?" *And how did you slip through the cracks?* he wanted to ask.

"Anyone who interviewed a candidate had to evaluate the person in terms of the company's values. When they talked about a potential new hire, they talked about the values. And during interviews, they asked behavioral questions to see if the candidate could cite examples that demonstrated that he or she fit the values."

Vince was silent, and Jamie tried to read his mind. "You're probably wondering why they hired me."

Vince shook his head, but was quietly hoping Jamie would answer the question. "Rich was on vacation," Jamie said. After a brief pause, the two men snorted with laughter.

Now fascinated by what he was learning, Vince persisted. "What about this other stuff? Roles and responsibilities? How did they deal with that?"

Jamie raised his eyebrows. "Now I have to admit that this part was pretty impressive. Rich would list the major objectives for each quarter on a board, and then he'd ask everyone to think of every possible thing that had to happen for each goal to be reached. When they had exhausted every activity, they divided them up among staff and began their individual goal-setting process there."

Vince made a few notes. "What happened when they didn't agree on the goals, or when someone didn't like the role they . . ."

Vince stopped himself when he saw Jamie pointing to discipline one. "Right."

Jamie continued. "As a result of the clarity they had around roles and responsibilities, things rarely slipped through the cracks, and people didn't step on each other's toes too often."

Out of nowhere Vince asked Jamie, "Can *you* help us do this?" He seemed desperate now.

Jamie was a little surprised by the pointed question. "Sure, I guess. If that's what you want to do. I'm sure you're doing most of this already."

Vince allowed himself a moment of self-preservational dishonesty. "Oh, yeah, we are. But this might be an interesting approach to try."

Jamie shrugged and nodded.

Suddenly Vince seemed skeptical again, as though he had just discovered a flaw in Telegraph's system. "Wait a second. So far all you've talked about is Telegraph's executive team. How does this stuff work its way into the rest of the organization?"

Jamie smiled. "That's where disciplines three and four come into play."

DISCIPLINE THREE

◯

Before Jamie could continue, Vince's phone rang. He picked up the receiver. "You're kidding." Vince looked over at Jamie with a smile of disbelief. "Yeah, put him through." After a brief pause, Vince greeted the caller: "How are you doing, Rich?"

Jamie hadn't yet digested the situation.

"Well, in fact, it has been a while, hasn't it?"

Suddenly it hit Jamie. Rich O'Connor was on the line. Vince could see the panic overtake Jamie. *Does Rich know I'm here?* Jamie thought. *This must be a setup. Shit.*

Vince ended the call. "Sure, I'll be around. I'll look forward to it. See you then." And he hung up. He seemed amused by Jamie's sudden loss of confidence. "What's the matter? Seen a ghost?" he teased.

Jamie was a little jumpy. "What's going on? How does he know I'm here?"

"Whoa. Slow down a little. First of all, nothing is going on. Rich has no idea that you're here."

"Is that normal for you to get a call from him?"

Vince laughed. "Only if you think that once every two or three years is normal." He could see Jamie squirm, so he offered a little reassurance. "Stop worrying, Jamie. You said it yourself: there is nothing preventing you from talking to me. Hell, they didn't even make you sign a noncompete clause. You're fine."

Jamie couldn't deny that Vince was correct. Still, something seemed wrong, and he persisted: "What did he want?"

"I'm not sure." Vince shrugged. "But it must be fairly important if he wants to see me." He seemed relieved to be receiving some of Rich's attention.

Jamie just sat there shaking his head.

With a new enthusiasm for learning about the final two disciplines, Vince prodded his guest. "Okay, let's talk about the next one."

It took Jamie a moment to regain his focus, and even then the first sentence out of his mouth sounded as if it was coming from someone in a daze. "Right. The third discipline is about communication." Jamie stopped, as if he were done explaining.

"Okay. What about communication?"

Jamie finally came around. "Oh, well, it's about communicating everything we just talked about. The clarity issues."

Vince tried to complete the thought. "You mean purpose and values and mission and objectives and all of that?"

"Right. The third discipline is 'Over-communicate the identity and direction.'"

"Over-communicate?" Vince frowned. "That sounds like something negative."

Jamie was nodding. "Yeah, that's what I thought when I first read it too. But I learned later that Rich thinks that in order to communicate something adequately, it has to be communicated so many times that the people doing the communication think they're beating a dead horse."

The look on Vince's face seemed to say, *That's weird.*

Jamie continued. "Remember how I said before that every member of Rich's team could recite, and with passion, all of the issues relating to clarity?"

Vince nodded.

"Well, that's because the guy says them over and over and over." Jamie seemed to suggest that Rich really was *over-communicating*. "And the thing is, he makes his entire team do the same thing with their people. And then he does it with the whole company too. I told you, the guy is obsessed."

"So how do they go about doing all this?"

Jamie took a deep breath, as if just thinking about the repetition was making him tired. "Well, first there's the orientation of new employees. I was lucky enough to miss out on his spiel, but Rich and a few members of his staff take two hours every other week to tell new employees about the history of the company, the values, the purpose, and everything else."

Vince wrote something down.

"But that's not all," Jamie continued. "Every time he gives a speech, or sends out an e-mail message, or even talks to a small group of people, he repeats this stuff."

Vince seemed doubtful. "Every time?"

"Well, not in exactly the same way, but he's constantly referring to it. It felt like listening to my grandfather tell the same stories over and over. But apparently no one over there seems to mind. They'd sit and give him their complete attention every time."

"And his staff does the same thing?"

"Not quite like Rich does, but they've definitely drunk the Kool-Aid."

Vince stared out the window, shaking his head slowly. Jamie assumed he was marveling at the ridiculousness of what he was hearing. He had no idea that Vince was beginning to understand.

Vince pushed the conversation forward. "Earlier you said something about posters. That Telegraph doesn't have any of this stuff on posters around the office?"

Jamie now seemed a little miffed as he considered the point. "That's right. As fanatical as they are about over-communicating, they would not let me have five thousand dollars to do a campaign around the company's values. I wanted to have some golf shirts done too, and make posters that we could use to spruce up their offices."

"Are you sure it was about the money?"

Jamie shook his head. "No, it was about Rich. He was adamant about not using anything slick or glossy, as he called it, to convey the identity of the company."

"Why do you suppose?" Vince wondered if Rich had become some sort of eccentric tyrant. He hoped he had.

"Rich always said that the minute you make any of this feel like a marketing campaign, it loses its—what was the word he used? It loses its 'groundedness.' He would say that 'it starts to feel like a slogan more than a reality.'"

At that moment, Jamie and Vince looked up at a framed poster on the wall above the conference table where they sat. It showed a fighter jet racing across the sky. In the background an enemy plane of some kind could be seen nose-diving toward the earth, smoke spewing from its tail. The caption below read, "SMARTER—BETTER—FASTER—GREENWICH." For a moment, Vince almost felt embarrassed, but he decided that would be a waste of his energy.

To break the awkward moment, Jamie stood, went to the white board and wrote down discipline three:

DISCIPLINE THREE: OVER-COMMUNICATE ORGANIZATIONAL CLARITY.

Vince looked down at his watch. "Okay then. Let's talk about the last discipline."

At that moment there was a knock at the door, and before Vince could respond, his assistant, Tracy, was already poking her head in. "Sorry to bother you, but Rich O'Connor's on his way up."

Jamie froze.

DISCIPLINE FOUR

"He's here right now?!" Jamie was incredulous. "You didn't say that he was coming today. Why didn't you tell . . ."

Vince laughed. "Calm down. He's going to find out sooner or later that you're interviewing here. This is a good chance for you to show me what you've got."

There was a knock at the door, and Tracy opened it before anyone answered. She showed Rich in and closed the door behind him.

Rich said "hi" to Vince and shook his hand, and then did a calm but unmistakable double-take when he saw his former vice president of human resources. "Well, hello there, Jamie."

Jamie was momentarily relieved to see that Rich did not expect him to be there. He was suddenly confident, standing and reaching out his hand to Rich. "Good to see you, Rich." But in spite of his controlled exterior, Jamie was a mess inside.

Rich smiled and turned to Vince. "Thanks for seeing me on such short notice. Can I talk to you for a few minutes?"

"Sure," Vince replied. He looked at Jamie. "Could you wait outside? Tracy will get you something to drink."

Rich added, in Jamie's direction. "This will only take a few minutes, if that."

"Take your time." Jamie smiled and headed for the door.

Once it had closed, Rich began: "I have a proposition for you, Vince." As always, Rich cut straight to the point.

"Aren't you a little curious about Jamie's being here?" Vince seemed pleased to have one of Rich's former employees in his office for a change.

Rich was unfazed. "I'm assuming he's interviewing for a job."

"He is. Should I hire him?"

Rich shrugged and smiled. "Well, my legal counsel would tell me that I'm not supposed to give out recommendations anymore, positive or negative. I guess these days people can sue you if you say the wrong thing."

They chuckled.

"But I will say this, Vince. Make sure you give him lots of support and direction. Jamie doesn't have the world's greatest sense of self-esteem, if you know what I mean."

Vince nodded, both to acknowledge the accuracy of Rich's assessment and to thank him for the advice. He was amazed that his adversary seemed completely comfortable with the notion that one of his recent senior staff members might join Greenwich.

"Anyway, what's your proposition?"

"I want to buy your retail practice. Tom tells me you have about ten clients and fifteen employees."

Vince was surprised that Rich knew anything about Greenwich. "That's pretty close. Why retail?"

"Well, we think it makes sense for us, given our strength in manufacturing and distribution. And I thought that rather than go through the process of staffing up an organization from scratch and fighting to take away your clients, we could talk about whether the retail market is important to you." Rich paused, hoping for some sort of clue as to the answer. "If it isn't, then I thought it might be easier for both of us if we did a deal. The market for good people is so tight, and that means I'd likely be recruiting some of your retail consultants anyway." Again he paused. "This just seems like it would be easier."

Vince couldn't decide if he were more amazed at Rich's candor or his confidence. *How can he just come right out and tell me, of all people, about his strategic intentions?* "Well, retail is not one of the vertical markets we see as a major part of our long-term strategy." *Why am I telling him this?* Rich's openness seemed to be contagious. "I'm curious to know why you think it is."

Rich smiled. "Now that's probably more information than we need to be sharing." They laughed.

"How many of my people would you want to take?"

"Well, that depends on how the interviews go. I'm guessing we'd hire at least half of them, if they're as good as we think they are."

"And how much money are we talking about?"

"I don't know." Rich genuinely seemed as though he had not thought about a number. "Maybe three times your annual revenue from retail. Does that seem fair?"

It was just enough for Vince to consider the deal, but not enough to make it an easy decision. "When do you need an answer?"

Rich thought about it. "I don't know. Two weeks?"

Vince agreed. "I'll call you." The rivals shook hands.

"Thanks, Vince." Rich looked out the office window and with the excitement of a twelve year old said, "That is one heck of a view."

Vince smiled. As hard as he tried, he could not detect even the slightest hint of sarcasm or condescension in his comment. For a moment Vince considered entertaining the notion that Rich might actually be more likable than the enemy he had constructed in his mind. Unwilling to challenge such a fundamental belief, however, he decided instead that his rival was probably holding something back.

Vince walked his guest to the door. As he opened it, Rich suddenly caught sight of the white board. He saw three of the four items from his list written in what looked like Jamie's handwriting.

Although Vince felt slightly embarrassed, more than anything he was curious to see how his rival would respond.

Facing toward the open door, Rich called Jamie in from the lobby.

As soon as he heard Rich's voice, Jamie remembered that he had failed to erase the white board.

When he arrived, Jamie immediately saw his former boss staring at the white board. He thought for a second that he was going to be sick.

Rich spoke first. "What is this?" His voice was without emotion.

Jamie stammered. "Well, I was just showing, uh, I mean I was explaining to Vince why the company, Telegraph I mean, has such a strong sense of . . ."

Mercifully, Rich interrupted. "Do you think this is right?"

Even Vince was beginning to get a little uncomfortable now. "Listen, it looks like you two need to talk. I'm going to leave you alone for a few minutes." He left the office, closing the door behind himself.

Jamie was about to spontaneously combust. "Well, I didn't think that it was necessarily a problem . . ."

Rich pretended not to hear Jamie's pathetic plea for mercy. He interrupted again. "Because you've got discipline two wrong." He walked to the white board and added *strategy* to the list that accompanied the second discipline. "If you don't get clear on the strategy piece, your goals and roles aren't going to be aligned."

Jamie was stunned with relief.

Out in the lobby, Vince was reading the *Wall Street Journal* and waiting for the conversation inside to end. After almost ten minutes, the door opened.

Rich came out first, looking calm. Jamie stood behind him, looking like a man who had just escaped a death experience.

Rich again shook Vince's hand. "Give me a call when you're ready to talk."

"Thanks, Rich."

Vince and Jamie watched Rich get into an elevator, and then they turned back toward the office.

Once inside, both men recited the same line simultaneously. "So?"

They both laughed nervously. Jamie recounted how the situation had been resolved.

Then Vince turned and saw the white board. The fourth discipline was now written there, but not in Jamie's handwriting:

DISCIPLINE FOUR: REINFORCE ORGANIZATIONAL CLARITY THROUGH HUMAN SYSTEMS.

He then noticed additional text on other parts of the board, written in this same script. It said:

BE COHESIVE.

BE CLEAR.

OVER-COMMUNICATE.

REINFORCE.

Vince struggled for words. "Did he write this?" He already knew the answer, but had to ask the question just to acknowledge the ridiculousness of the situation.

Jamie nodded his head, and motioned toward the white board. "Yeah, he filled in part of discipline two here, added the fourth one, and wrote an abbreviated version of all four that he said is easier to remember."

The two men stared at the board, shaking their heads.

"I told you," said Jamie, "the guy's nuts." As relieved as he was, he could still not bring himself to be completely gracious toward Rich.

Refocusing after the episode, Jamie and Vince sat down again at the conference table. Vince began: "So?"

"So what?"

"Are you going to explain the fourth discipline to me?"

Laughing, as if to say, *What else are we going to do?* Jamie began. He repeated the discipline. "'Reinforce organizational clarity through human systems.' This one is the most important in terms of preserving the other three."

Vince was having a hard time listening. After the encounter with Rich, his excitement about the list and its importance seemed to have diminished somewhat. Rich no longer seemed like a mysterious figure in Vince's eyes, but rather an ordinary man obsessed with a basic philosophy. In fact, Vince felt almost ashamed about his excitement around learning Rich's secrets. *This isn't so hard,* he thought to himself. Vince gladly welcomed back his sense of superiority and contempt.

With a new air of skepticism, he said, "Sorry, Jamie, I just don't get this last one."

"Well, Rich would say that this one is about building a structure and a system to preserve Telegraph's culture. He used to say that 'culture lives in the way things get done.' Or something like that."

"You mean like operations? Business policies?"

"Not exactly. Remember, the structure he's thinking about has to do with *human* systems and operations—things like interviewing and hiring people, managing their performance, rewarding them, and," Jamie almost winced before finishing the sentence, "letting them go."

Vince was still intent on getting more information, but now in a way that seemed to be challenging the validity of the concepts. "We do all of those things. How is Telegraph any different?"

"Well, first there are those damn interviews." Jamie's contempt made Vince curious.

"What do they do?"

"What *don't* they do?" he complained. "They put every candidate through at least five interviews. They insist on using a core set of behavioral questions, asked in slightly different ways by different people. And then they make all the interviewers get together in a room and debrief." Jamie paused. "They do this for vice presidents, consultants, even receptionists."

"You mean interviewers can't ask their own questions?"

"Well, they can, but they have to spend so much time on the behavioral stuff that it makes the process seem like work." Jamie recognized the ironic nature of the comment, given his career choice. "I mean, it shouldn't have been so hard. It was just too structured."

Vince smiled. "You really hated it, didn't you?"

"Well, I guess it was because I had to enforce the system. And whenever I tried to change it, they stopped me. I thought I should get to decide how to go about staffing the organization."

Vince frowned. "What else?"

"You mean about interviewing?"

"No. I think I've got it. What about . . ."

Jamie interrupted him. "Performance management. That was another part of my responsibility. I had to make sure that every manager, at every level, did a quarterly management report for each of their people. It was a nightmare."

Vince laughed. "Yeah, you were probably bugging the hell out of everyone trying to get all their forms in on time."

Jamie shook his head. "No, pretty much everyone did their forms on time. It was only one page with three simple questions on it, and no one complained about it, at least not to me."

Vince was surprised. "One page? Come on."

Jamie thought about it. "Well, I guess it was more than that."

Vince seemed pleased, as though he had been vindicated in some way, until Jamie explained: "There was a question on the back too, but just for discussion. So I guess you could say that it was two pages."

Vince's vindication disappeared. "Okay, so what were these questions? I don't suppose there were four?"

Jamie laughed. "Actually there *were* four."

The two men shook their heads as if to say, *That is one weird company.* Vince motioned for Jamie to tell him more.

"The questions were, 'What did you accomplish?' 'What will you accomplish next?' 'How can you improve?'"

"That's it?"

"Not quite. The question on the back was, 'Are you embracing the values?'"

"So why was this such a nightmare for you?"

"Because I hated doing those things for my employees and having Rich do it for me."

"How long could it take to fill out a one-page form?"

"Longer than you think, because everyone takes it so seriously. But it wasn't filling out the form that was the problem. It was the follow-up discussion."

Before Vince could ask, Jamie explained. "Every manager had to spend ninety minutes in a room with each of his employees, going over the report."

"Didn't they run out of things to talk about? Ninety minutes is a long time."

"That's the funny part. Rich used to say that he wanted people to run out of things to talk about. Because that was when they would start talking about the important things." Jamie shook his head. "He's an odd bird."

"So people actually did this? They spent ninety minutes together, with every direct report, every quarter?"

Jamie nodded his head as if to say, "Unbelievable, isn't it?"

"Well, they must not be busy enough over there if they can waste that much time doing management reviews." Vince seemed to be regaining his confidence and losing his interest in the magic of Rich O'Connor. He stood up and stretched his arms. "It's no wonder they're not growing faster. I think I've heard enough."

Jamie frowned. "What did you say?"

"I've heard enough. But I appreciate your taking the time . . ."

Jamie interrupted him. "No, before that. You said something about their growth?"

"Yeah, I've often wondered why they haven't grown faster. For all of their supposed advantages, we're still almost as big as they are."

Jamie's demeanor suddenly changed. He seemed stunned, but in an almost sad kind of way. "Hmm."

Vince noticed the change. "What do you mean 'hmm'?"

"I think you better sit down."

THE REALIZATION

○

Vince was not about to sit down. "Why?"

Jamie smiled, not so much amused as surprised and concerned. "So you really don't know why they aren't bigger?"

"Well, I don't think they're as good as we are at winning business. I mean, whenever it comes down to a head-to-head competition between us and them in the final stages of bidding, they win most of the time. But it seems that more often than not, they don't even get to the final round. They just disappear after the first round of discussions."

"That's it?" Jamie asked.

"Well, I do think they waste a lot of time on all of this internal stuff, and that has to detract from their ability to grow more aggressively. No one has that kind of time to waste these days."

Jamie knew that he was going to have to break the news to him, and Vince sensed this. "What? What am I missing?"

Vince finally sat down, and Jamie leaned forward in his chair. "Vince, they *are* growing as fast as they want to grow." He paused, but Vince didn't understand, so he continued. "They hit their revenue and profitability targets on the nose almost every quarter."

"So?"

"Vince, they turn away more business than they take. Rich doesn't *want* to grow any faster right now."

Revelation was just beginning to show on Vince's face, so Jamie went on. "They disappear in the first round of those situations because they opt out. They only take on clients that they want to take on. You get most of those deals by default."

And then Jamie delivered the final blow: "Telegraph is not trying to be bigger than you. They aren't competing that way."

Vince leaned back in his chair, in disbelief. Jamie wanted to enjoy having the upper hand, but he couldn't deny that he felt sorry for Vince. He looked like a broken man.

PART FOUR

The Resolution

THE DECISION

○

Over the course of the next two weeks, Vince experienced a struggle within himself about whether he would embrace or reject Rich O'Connor's methodology. Rejection won.

After disparaging his rival for so long, he did not have the strength to suddenly change course and let the success of his own firm rest on the ideas of a competitor. Vince decided that he would win on his own terms, so he politely rejected Rich's offer to purchase the retail division, and dedicated himself more than ever to growing the firm.

During the months that followed, Vince experienced sporadic periods of disappointment and frustration, especially when he saw examples of how his firm was not measuring up to Telegraph and its approach. For a while, he learned to ignore these feelings, but over time they began to haunt him.

Vince could not bear to spend time with his undeniably dysfunctional executive team, and the lack of any sense of culture or values became increasingly apparent. To make matters worse, during moments of weakness he suspected that relief might be just four disciplines away.

But even if he believed in them, those disciplines didn't seem accessible to Vince. After all, he didn't go into business so he could referee executive team meetings and deliver employee orientation. Vince loved strategy and competition, and that was it. He certainly didn't have the stomach for focusing his energy on something as soft and uncertain as organizational health.

For the first time in his career, Vince felt he was losing his passion for business. He never thought that he would even consider what he was about to do.

WHITE FLAG

J ust two months and three weeks after coming to terms with his decision, the deal was complete. Vince Green had sold the firm he had founded almost ten years earlier. Although he had offered it to his rival, he knew that Rich would decline. So instead, the firm was swallowed up by a large East Coast consulting firm.

Within a year, Vince grew bored and started another firm, this time a software company. Although he had worried about whether he would be able to reestablish his passion for business, he found that the fresh start, coupled with a new openness about the four disciplines, gave him just the energy he needed.

During this same time, Rich decided to grow Telegraph at a quicker pace than before, partly by acquiring a few specialty consulting firms. Within three years, the firm had doubled in size, and Rich became less involved in client-related work than ever before. Instead, he found that he needed to spend even more time on the four disciplines in order to maintain the success of his now larger firm.

However, there was one client, GreenWare Systems, that Rich took special interest in whenever he had time. In fact, he even accepted the CEO's invitation to sit on its board of directors.

As for Jamie, he was now working for a rival consulting firm, heading the HR department. Tom often joked that Telegraph would have gladly paid the recruiter a finder's fee for landing him the job.

Rich surprised himself by quietly hoping that Jamie would find a way to succeed.

AFTERWORD

hy did Rich O'Connor succeed? Some would say that he was an extraordinary man. I'm not so sure.

While Rich certainly had a number of amazing qualities, in many ways he was a quite ordinary man. He had faults and problems like anyone else. It was his appreciation for simplicity and discipline that made him an extraordinary executive.

This is good news for all of us who don't quite measure up to Rich just yet. There is hope for us because we too can become extraordinary leaders if we only embrace the fact that success is not so much a function of intelligence or natural ability, but rather of commitment to the right disciplines.

But there is the potential for bad news here too. We can become poor leaders, more like Vince, or even Jamie, if we let ourselves become distracted by overly tactical and political matters.

The choice is ours to make. Every day.

Organizational Health

⬯

The Model

PUTTING THE DISCIPLINES INTO PRACTICE
A Summary and Self-Assessment

$$\bigcirc$$

Most executives spend considerable time and energy in search of competitive advantage, usually in areas like strategy, technology, marketing, and other fields that are based on intellectual property or capital. This is smart.

Unfortunately, the ubiquity and flow of information has reduced the sustainability of these types of advantages such that companies enjoy shorter periods of differentiation than ever before. This trend will certainly continue, and most likely it will accelerate.

However, there is one competitive advantage that is available to any company that wants it and yet is largely ignored. What is more, it is as sustainable as it has ever been because it is not based on information or intellectual property at all. What I am referring to is something I call organizational health, and it occupies a lot of the time and attention of extraordinary executives.

A healthy organization is one that has less politics and confusion, higher morale and productivity, lower unwanted turnover, and lower recruiting costs than an unhealthy one. No leader I know would dispute the power of these qualities, and every one of them would love his or her organization to have them. Unfortunately, most executives struggle with how to go about making this happen.

The first step is to embrace the idea that, like so many other aspects of success, organizational health is simple in theory but difficult to put into practice. It requires extraordinary levels of commitment, courage and consistency. However, it does not require complex thinking and analysis; in fact, keeping things simple is critical. It can even be summarized on a single page (see facing page).

The second step is to master these fundamental disciplines and put them into practice on a daily basis. The remainder of this book is dedicated to helping you understand how to do just that.

DISCIPLINE ONE:
BUILD AND MAINTAIN A COHESIVE LEADERSHIP TEAM

Building a cohesive leadership team is the most critical of the four disciplines because it enables the other three. It is also the most elusive because it requires considerable interpersonal commitment from an executive team and its leader.

The Four Disciplines of a Healthy Organization

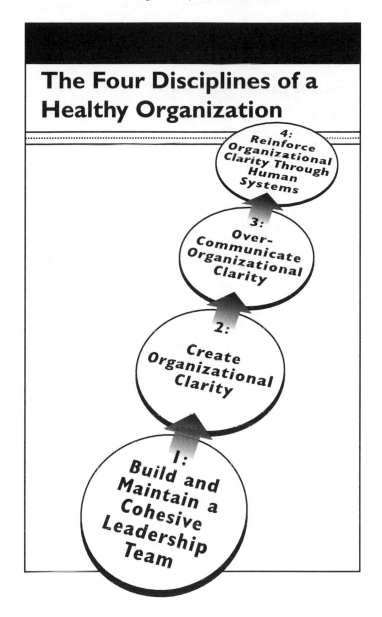

Discipline 1:

Build and Maintain a Cohesive Leadership Team

Cohesive teams build trust, eliminate politics, and increase efficiency by ...

Knowing one another's unique strengths and weaknesses

Openly engaging in constructive ideological conflict

Holding one another accountable for behaviors and actions

Committing to group decisions

Reinforce Organizational Clarity Through Human Systems

Over-Communicate Organizational Clarity

Create Organizational Clarity

Build and Maintain a Cohesive Leadership Team

The essence of a cohesive leadership team is trust, which is marked by an absence of politics, unnecessary anxiety, and wasted energy. Every executive wants to achieve this, but few are able to do so because they fail to understand the roots of these problems, the most damaging of which is politics.

Politics is the result of unresolved issues at the highest level of an organization, and attempting to curb politics without addressing issues at the executive level is pointless. Although most executives I've worked with are aware of the existence of some political behavior within their teams, they almost always underestimate its magnitude and the impact it has on the company and its people.

This blindness occurs because what executives believe are small disconnects between themselves and their peers actually look like major rifts to people deeper in the organization. And when those people deeper in the organization try to resolve the differences among themselves, they often become engaged in bloody and time-consuming battles, with no possibility for resolution. And all of this occurs because leaders higher in the organization failed to work out minor issues, usually out of fear of conflict.

The commonness and severity of this problem make the point worth repeating. When an executive decides not to confront a peer about a potential disagreement, he or she is dooming employees to waste time, money, and emotional energy dealing with unresolvable issues. This causes the best employees to start looking for jobs in less dysfunctional organizations, and it creates an environment of disillusionment, distrust, and exhaustion for those who stay.

Cohesive leadership teams, on the other hand, resolve their issues and create environments of trust for themselves, and thus for their people. They ensure that most of the energy expended in the organization is focused on achieving the desired results of the firm. What is more, I have found that outstanding employees rarely leave these organizations.

What Does a Cohesive Leadership Team Look Like?

More than anything else, cohesive teams are efficient. They arrive at decisions more quickly and with greater buy-in than non-cohesive teams do. They also spend less time worrying about whether their peers will commit to a plan and deliver.

One of the best ways to recognize a cohesive team is the nature of its meetings. Passionate. Intense. Exhausting. Never boring.

For cohesive teams, meetings are compelling and vital. They are forums for asking difficult questions, challenging one another's ideas, and ultimately arriving at decisions that everyone agrees to support and adhere to, in the best interests of the company.

Within the cohesive teams that I work with, members hold their peers accountable for behaviors that are not conducive to team performance. No one reads e-mail or does ancillary busywork during meetings, even when the issue on the table is not directly related to them. Everyone is involved and awake. If an issue hits the agenda and it is not compelling or critical, team members question whether it is worth their time.

Finally, cohesive teams fight. But they fight about issues, not personalities. Most important, when they are done fighting, they have an amazing capacity to move on to the next issue, with no residual feelings.

In those instances when a fight gets out of hand and drifts over the line into personal territory—and this inevitably happens—the entire team works to make things right. No one walks away from a meeting harboring unspoken resentment.

Unfortunately, many executive teams never achieve this. They yearn for easy, peaceful staff meetings as a retreat from their hectic schedules. What they end up getting are tedious and uninspiring show-and-tell sessions where department heads review the details of their responsibilities.

Is achieving cohesiveness difficult? Sure. A better question would be, "Is it worth the effort?" Whether you measure the results in terms of increased productivity, reduced turnover, higher quality of worklife, or simply less time in unproductive meetings, the answer is always a resounding yes.

How Is a Cohesive Leadership Team Built?

The most important activity is the building of trust, and one of the best ways to do this is what I call "getting naked." This is not a New Age exercise involving group hugs and holding hands, but rather a general process of getting to know one another at a level that few groups of people—unfortunately, even many families—ever achieve.

There are many effective ways to get naked. No single method is enough, but none is specifically required. What is most important is that team members get comfortable letting their colleagues see them for who they are. No pretension. No positioning.

Although there are certainly unstructured approaches to building a cohesive team, I suggest taking a look at some of the proven methods and philosophies first.

• Myers-Briggs Type Indicator. Often referred to as the MBTI, this is a profoundly effective tool for helping team members understand one another's behaviors and avoid dangerous misattributions. It has been tested and used by millions of people, and there is no shortage of material relating to applying it to teams. I have found that even the most skeptical executive teams find significant, lasting benefit from using this tool.

• *The Wisdom of Teams*. Jon Katzenbach and Douglas Smith wrote one of the most compelling, no-nonsense approaches to building teams that I have seen. *The Wisdom of Teams* (and its companion volume, *Teams at the Top*) outlines the basic requirements for real teamwork and high-performing teams.

- *The Five Temptations of a CEO.* I wrote this book to help members of a leadership team self-identify their temptations and discuss how they might go about addressing them in the context of the team. It provides unique insights into the strengths and weaknesses of colleagues, especially as they relate to leadership within the context of an organization.

- Personal histories. Although it might sound like a "touchy-feely" exercise, I have found that it is remarkably helpful for members of a leadership team to spend time talking about their backgrounds. People who understand one another's personal philosophies, family histories, educational experiences, hobbies, and interests are far more likely to work well together than those who do not. And given the large portion of our lives spent at work, getting to know peers on a meaningful level can go a long way toward making work fulfilling.

Now, achieving cohesiveness does not happen only during an off site meeting or on a fixed schedule. In fact, a key part of building trust is about living through difficult times. Like a marriage or any other meaningful relationship, the only way to build strength is to share experiences that require everyone to rally and overcome obstacles. The most cohesive teams I know have faced ugly issues and even come dangerously close to dissolution. But by surviving, they develop a level of trust that is hard to break. The key for a leader is to remind team members why difficult times are worth tolerating, and what the rewards will be.

Once a team has achieved some level of cohesiveness, its ability to maintain it rests on its willingness to continually address core issues, and its discipline around having regular, frequent, and in-person meetings. While travel schedules and demanding workloads make it more and more difficult to get together regularly, it is nevertheless critical that an executive team not give in to the temptation to scale back meetings. Failing to honor meeting schedules, something that is all too common in most organizations, is the first sign that a leadership team is about to experience problems.

In terms of the effectiveness of a particular team, my experience indicates that a group's cohesiveness has far more impact on success than its collective level of experience or knowledge. I have worked with leadership teams filled with industry luminaries and accomplished executives who could not compete with less experienced and relatively unknown teams that were able to create environments of trust and passion. Quite simply, cohesiveness at the executive level is the single greatest indicator of future success that any organization can achieve.

How Do You Assess Your Team for Cohesiveness?

Ask yourself these questions:

- *Are meetings compelling? Are the important issues being discussed during meetings?*

Every company has interesting, difficult issues to wrestle with, and a lack of interest during meetings is a pretty good indication that the team may be avoiding issues because they are uncomfortable with one another. Remember, there is no excuse for having continually boring meetings.

- *Do team members engage in unguarded debate? Do they honestly confront one another?*

Every executive team should be engaged and passionate about what it does, regardless of its business. Even teams that get along well together should be experiencing regular conflict and intense debate during meetings.

If this is not the case, it is likely that there is a lack of trust, and an unwillingness to confront one another. Even the best teams have moments when members need to hold one another accountable for their attitudes or actions. Holding back during these times is a sure sign of future problems for the team.

- *Do team members apologize if they get out of line? Do they ever get out of line?*

When people confront one another, discomfort inevitably occurs. Sometimes people get emotional; sometimes they say things they don't mean. When this happens, it is key that they are comfortable apologizing to one another. As soft as it may seem, teams that can genuinely forgive and ask forgiveness develop powerful levels of trust.

- *Do team members understand one another?*

Members of cohesive teams know one another's strengths and weaknesses and don't hesitate to point them out. They also know something about one another's backgrounds, which helps them to understand why members think and act the way they do.

- *Do team members avoid gossiping about one another?*

Talking about a colleague who is not present is not gossip. Gossip requires the intent to hurt someone, and it is almost always accompanied by an unwillingness to confront a person directly with the information being discussed. Ironically, members of cohesive teams are not overly concerned about the prospect of their colleagues' discussing them in their absence because they know it is in the best interest of the team. They trust each other, and know that true gossip will not be tolerated.

If you answered no to any of these questions, you may have identified an opportunity to make your team more cohesive. The best way to begin this process is to discuss the questions presented here with the members of your team and ask them what their answers would be. Getting members to agree on which of these issues is most challenging for the team is the first step toward addressing it.

DISCIPLINE TWO: CREATE ORGANIZATIONAL CLARITY

Most executives profess to understand the importance of creating clarity in their organizations, but ironically, they often fail to achieve it. Maybe that's because it is deceptively familiar.

After all, management consultants and strategy experts have been talking about mission statements, goals, objectives, and values for years, spawning a cottage industry of poster makers who decorate corporate hallways with vacuous statements about customers, quality, and teamwork.

But organizational clarity is not merely about choosing the right words to describe a company's mission, strategy, or values; it is about agreeing on the fundamental concepts that drive it.

Why is this so important? Because it provides employees at all levels of an organization with a common vocabulary and set of assumptions about what is important and what is not. More important, it allows them to make decisions and resolve problems without constant supervision and advice from managers. Essentially, organizational clarity allows a company to delegate more effectively and empower its employees with a true sense of confidence.

Discipline 2:

Create Organizational Clarity

A healthy organization minimizes the potential for confusion by clarifying . . .

Why the organization exists

Which behavioral values are fundamental

What specific business it is in

Who its competitors are

How it is unique

What it plans to achieve

Who is responsible for what

Reinforce Organizational Clarity Through Human Systems

Over-Communicate Organizational Clarity

Create Organizational Clarity

Build and Maintain a Cohesive Leadership Team

What Does Organizational Clarity Look Like?

An organization that has achieved clarity has a sense of unity around everything it does. It aligns its resources, especially the human ones, around common concepts, values, definitions, goals, and strategies, thereby realizing the synergies that all great companies must achieve.

The result is an undeniable sense of focus and efficiency, concepts that even the most quantitatively oriented leader can embrace. When employees at all levels share a common understanding of where the company is headed, what success looks like, whom their competitors are, and what needs to be achieved to claim victory, there is a remarkably low level of wasted time and energy and a powerful sense of traction.

Employees in these organizations seem to have amazing levels of autonomy. They know what their boundaries are and when they need guidance from management before taking action. Their ability to make decisions for themselves creates an environment of empowerment, traction, and urgency.

If this is so powerful, then why don't all executives create clarity in their organizations? Because many of them overemphasize the value of flexibility. Wanting their organizations to be "nimble," they hesitate to articulate their direction clearly, or do so in a less than thorough manner, thus giving themselves the deceptively dangerous luxury of changing plans in midstream.

Ironically, truly nimble organizations dare to create clarity at all times, even when they are not completely certain about whether it is correct. And if they later see a need to change course, they do so without hesitation or apology, and thus create clarity around the new idea or answer.

Behaviorally, achieving real clarity in an organization requires an executive team to demonstrate commitment and courage. The teams I have worked with that do this are not necessarily smarter than their competitors, nor are they more experienced within their industries. However, they are definitely less afraid of being wrong.

So, as common as mission and vision statements are in most companies, few organizations achieve real clarity. This is unfortunate because clarity provides power like nothing else can. It establishes a foundation for communication, hiring, training, promotion, and decision making, and serves as the basis for accountability in an organization, which is a requirement for long-term success.

How Does an Organization Go About Achieving Clarity?

One of the best ways to achieve clarity is to answer, in no uncertain terms, a series of basic questions pertaining to the organization:

- Why does the organization exist, and what difference does it make in the world?

- What behavioral values are irreplaceable and fundamental?
- What business are we in, and against whom do we compete?
- How does our approach differ from that of our competition?
- What are our goals this month, this quarter, this year, next year, five years from now?
- Who has to do what for us to achieve our goals this month, this quarter, this year, next year, five years from now?

While some of these questions might seem esoteric and others tactical, all of them are important. The key is that at any given point in time, a healthy organization can point to an unambiguous answer for each question. Without those answers, confusion and hesitation begin to invade an organization.

One key to achieving organizational clarity is focusing on the essence of each question and not getting bogged down by the temptation to wordsmith the answers. Executive teams often lapse into "marketing mode" while discussing clarity, and start thinking about creating external marketing messages and tag lines rather than getting agreement around the basic concepts themselves.

In addition to this general distraction, each of the questions carries its own unique challenges, which are explored in detail in this section.

Why Does the Organization Exist, and What Difference Does It Make in the World? The challenge with this question is convincing a skeptical executive team that its answer has relevance for the organization and for the daily activities of employees. Though it may at first seem esoteric, it sets the stage for almost every decision the organization makes.

A successful Internet consulting firm I work with claims that it exists to help people realize their ideas. It believes that it makes a difference in the world by bringing start-up companies to life and giving people opportunities to work and invent new ways of doing business. As nice as this may sound, it is valuable only because the firm uses it to guide many of its decisions. When the company acquired two smaller firms, it chose them because they shared its enthusiasm for realizing dreams. When it evaluates new projects, job applicants, new markets, and new strategies, it always asks itself whether there is a fit with its underlying reason for being. The executive team attributes much of its success to the clarity it has achieved around why the company exists and its ability to adhere to it over time.

A clear explanation of this general principle comes from the work of Jerry Porras and Jim Collins in their book *Built to Last*. They describe the concept in detail and provide examples of companies that were able to articulate their core reason for being, as well as their core values, which is the focus of the next question.

What Behavioral Values Are Irreplaceable and Fundamental? The key to answering this question lies in avoiding the tendency to adopt every positive value that exists. Many companies I've worked with want to claim that they are equally committed to quality, innovation, teamwork, ethics, integrity, customer satisfaction, employee development, financial results, and community involvement. Although all of these qualities are certainly desirable and might even exist in a single company at a given time, the search for fundamental values requires a significant level of focus and introspection, and a willingness to acknowledge that all things good are not necessarily essential to an organization.

In fact, the healthiest organizations identify a small set of values that are particularly fundamental to their culture, and adhere to those values without exception. It is not that they reject all other values, but rather that they know which qualities lie at the heart of whom they are. This knowledge makes decision making easier and gives employees, customers, and shareholders an accurate picture of what the company represents.

In *Built to Last,* Porras and Collins provide many examples of how companies identify and use core values to guide the decisions they make. They make a point that I believe is worth repeating here: fundamental values are not chosen from thin air based on the desires of executives; they are discovered within what already exists in an organization.

One way that I help executive teams identify their fundamental values is by asking them to think about the two or three employees whom they believe best embody what is good about the firm. These would be people whom they would gladly clone again and again, regardless of their responsibility or level of experience. Then I ask them to write down one or two adjectives that describe the employees they selected. Usually a relatively short list of common or related terms surfaces.

To help them solidify their thinking, I then ask them to identify the one or two employees who have left the firm, or should leave the firm, because of their behavior or performance. Coming up with these names never seems to take long. Again, I ask them to write down one or two adjectives that describe the people they chose. Almost without fail, the same adjectives appear on most team members' lists, and these often embody the antithesis of the company's fundamental values.

Another approach to identifying values involves focusing on the common behavioral values of the people who founded the organization. This can be particularly useful in relatively new companies where there is little opportunity to reflect on past and current employees.

Now, the wrong way to determine an organization's values is to survey the employee population. This may seem to be a useful way to test a hypothesis, but it is not a replacement for the introspection and discussion of an executive team. More important, it can lead to the adoption of a value set that executives are not willing to support.

These are just a few ways that an executive team can go about identifying its values. Whatever method is used, it is important to remember that the process should not be hurried, and initial answers should be tested and reality-checked before being communicated to the organization at large.

What Business Are We in, and Against Whom Do We Compete? I believe that a company cannot be called great if virtually every employee, and certainly every executive, cannot articulate the basic definition of what the company does. As simple as this seems, it is common to encounter employees in most companies who are not sure how to describe or define their organization's basic mission.

By the way, that word *mission* often creates confusion. Some people think a mission is a lofty statement of ideals, others define it as an organizational goal, and still others call it a business definition. I recommend that any organization that shares this confusion stop using the term altogether and come up with a different term instead.

Whatever term it chooses, a company needs to be able to articulate exactly what it does, whom it serves, and against whom it competes. Why? Because all employees should be made to feel like salespeople or ambassadors for the firm, and they cannot do this without a fundamental understanding of an organization's business. More important, without this understanding, employees cannot connect their individual roles to the overall direction of the larger organization.

How Does Our Approach Differ from That of Our Competition? Essentially this is a strategy question. Most companies I have encountered have different ways of defining and approaching strategy. Unfortunately, in spite of the fact that strategy is such a popular topic within business schools and in business media, there is no clear and simple definition of what it means.

I believe that an organization's strategy comprises nothing and everything. By that I mean that no single concept can summarize a company's strategy, yet every decision that a company makes contributes to or is a function of its strategy.

Take Southwest Airlines, for instance. If you were to ask most people what SWA's strategy is, they would claim one of the following: low fares, on-time arrivals and departures, great service, regional routes. Give them a few more minutes and they'll add more to the list: no frills, no first class, no preassigned seating, and humorous flight attendants who wear shorts. Which of these many attributes, all of which are true by the way, make up Southwest's strategy? They all do.

Certainly the first few would be considered the company's strategic anchors, but every decision that the airline makes, even allowing its employees to wear shorts, is connected to the strategy. And what is more, it is the collection of those decisions that differentiates Southwest from other airlines. Low fares alone does not differentiate them. On-time performance doesn't either. But by combining these qualities with the others, it becomes very clear that Southwest has chosen a strategy that sets it apart from its competitors. Every organization should be able to be so clear.

The key is taking the time to look at all of the decisions that the company has made, even the obvious ones, and identify those that, when combined, make the company uniquely positioned for success.

What Are Our Goals This Month, This Quarter, This Year, Next Year, Five Years from Now? Because of the inconsistent use of the term, *goals* present organizations with another problem. That is why it is important to distinguish different types of goals from one another and use terms that eliminate confusion.

At the highest level, an organization should have one or two basic *thematic goals* for a given period. These might include survival, efficiency, professionalism, or growth. Whatever it is, the purpose of a thematic goal is to rally employees, regardless of their specific jobs, around a common direction. A good way to arrive at a thematic goal is to finish the following sentence: "This is the year that our organization will . . ."

Beneath a thematic goal there should be *major strategic goals* that span the organization and support its overall theme. For instance, if an organization's thematic goal is growth, then its major strategic goals might include increasing revenue, adding new customers, hiring new employees, expanding to new sites, increasing market awareness, and improving infrastructure. If the thematic goal were survival, the categories might be achieving financial stability, retaining employees, retaining customers, and improving public relations.

Like so many other aspects of clarity, the key here is to focus on the areas that matter most and to avoid making every possible topic an area of equal importance. For example, even a company that is growing needs to retain its employees. However, employee acquisition may be the most relevant category to focus on and deserves more attention. Similarly, a company in survival mode certainly is interested in acquiring new customers, but it may want to place customer retention under a brighter spotlight for a given period.

Within each of these goals, an organization must be explicit. How many new customers? By when? From which regions? Getting specific about exactly what needs to be achieved, even in the face of uncertainty, is one mark of a healthy organization.

Finally, strategic goals need to be aligned with an organization's permanent measures of success, which are *metrics*. For instance, virtually every organization should constantly have quantitative objectives related to permanent topics like revenue, expenses, profit, employee turnover, employee satisfaction, and productivity. These objectives become the means for keeping score over time and for evaluating the success of the actions within each of the thematic categories.

Many organizations make the mistake of using metrics in place of thematic and strategic goals. This is a problem because metrics do not inspire enthusiasm among employees, nor do they align behaviors around common themes or strategies.

Here, in summary, are the levels of goals that healthy organizations must embrace:

Thematic goals:	What is this period's focus?
Major strategic goals:	What are the key areas which relate to that focus, and exactly what needs to be achieved?
Metrics:	What are the ongoing measures that allow the organization to keep score?

Once an organization has clarified these areas, it can call on its various departments to build their own goals, in a manner that is aligned with the direction of the entire organization. This requires that an executive team set its goals relatively early and avoid the temptation to waffle about what it wants the organization to achieve.

Who Has to Do What for Us to Achieve Our Goals for This Month, This Quarter, This Year, Next Year, Five Years from Now? One of the greatest problems that organizations encounter when it comes to achieving clarity is the inability to translate company goals into concrete responsibilities for members of an executive team. As fundamental as this activity would seem, most organizations don't do a good job of breaking down their goals into clear deliverables for team members. This is partly due to the fact that they make dangerous assumptions about roles based on people's titles, and because they shy away from difficult territorial conversations about who is truly responsible for what.

Every executive has his or her own preconceived notions about the difference between a sales vice president and a marketing vice president. However, when it comes time to assign responsibilities for specific goals, it is necessary to throw those assumptions out the window and look at each situation in terms of who would be the most appropriate owner, and why.

In some cases, roles are unclear because executive teams begin the process of establishing individual responsibilities before organizational goals have been set. The key to avoiding this situation is to take the strategic goals that have been set for the organization and then ask, "What has to happen in order for us to achieve each goal?" Each strategic goal will have many subgoals, and ownership for each of those should be explicit.

Only when each goal is broken down into components and ownership has been assigned to appropriate executives can accountability be achieved. When a goal might seem to be the responsibility of a collection of executives, it is still necessary to designate one person as the owner of that goal. Without clear ownership, accountability becomes difficult, even within the best teams.

It is worth repeating here that one of the keys to achieving clarity in this area is the willingness to engage in constructive conflict about who is best suited for which roles, and to sustain that conflict until agreement has been reached. This applies to every other area of clarity too. As you can imagine, without discipline one, this is virtually impossible.

How Do You Assess Your Organization for Clarity?

This is pretty simple. Ask your team members to individually answer the questions set out in this section. It is useful to have them write their answers down. Then go around the table and have everyone report their answers to the rest of the team. Fundamental differences will be painfully apparent. Keep in mind that it is okay for people to use slightly different language when they answer the various questions. What you are looking for is conceptual agreement.

DISCIPLINE THREE:
OVER-COMMUNICATE ORGANIZATIONAL CLARITY

Once the executive team has achieved clarity, it must then communicate that clarity to employees. This is the simplest of the four disciplines, but tragically, the most underachieved. Why is this tragic? Because after having done all the work associated with disciplines one and two, it is a shame not to reap the benefits of those achievements. Especially when it is so simple.

What Does Over-Communication Look Like?

Within companies that effectively over-communicate, employees at all levels and in all departments understand what the organization is about and how they contribute to its success. They don't spend time speculating on what executives are really thinking, and they don't look for hidden messages among the information they receive. As a result, there is a strong sense of common purpose and direction, which supersedes any departmental or ideological allegiances they may have.

Employees in healthy organizations may joke, or sometimes even complain, about the volume and repetition of information that they receive. But they'll be glad that they are not being kept in the dark about what is going on.

Discipline 3:

Over-Communicate Organizational Clarity

Healthy organizations align their employees around organizational clarity by communicating key messages through ...

Repetition: Don't be afraid to repeat the same message, again and again.

Simplicity: The more complicated the message, the more potential for confusion and inconsistency.

Multiple Mediums: People react to information in many ways; use a variety of mediums.

Cascading Messages: Leaders communicate key messages to direct reports; the cycle repeats itself until the message is heard by all.

Reinforce Organizational Clarity Through Human Systems

Over-Communicate Organizational Clarity

Create Organizational Clarity

Build and Maintain a Cohesive Leadership Team

How Does an Executive Team Effectively Over-Communicate?

The first step is to embrace the three most critical practices of effective organizational communication: repetition, simple messages, and multiple mediums. Ironically, these have nothing to do with presentation style or speaking ability.

Repetition. The issue here has to do with the fear of repetition. Most executives I work with don't like to repeat the same message again and again over time. This is because they are relatively intelligent people who don't want to underestimate the intelligence of their audience. And so they make the dangerous assumption that once a message has been heard, it is both understood and embraced by employees.

Other executives complain about repetition because they are bored with a message after communicating it once or twice, and want to move on to solve the next problem within the organization. They enjoy the problem solving and find little intellectual stimulation in repetitive communication.

Unfortunately, effective communication requires repetition in order to take hold in an organization. Some experts say that only after hearing a message six times does a person begin to believe and internalize it. Even if that number is just three, consider how many times an executive would have to communicate a message before every employee in the organization will have heard it three times.

This problem is extremely common in organizations where I have worked. Almost without exception, executives lament having to repeat the same "tired" messages. In the next breath, they complain that employees are not hearing and acting on the messages they communicate.

One of the keys to successful communication, I remind them, is getting used to saying the same things again and again, to different audiences, and in slightly different ways. Whether they are bored with those messages is not the issue; whether employees understand and embrace them is.

Simple Messages. Another key to effective communication is the ability to avoid overcomplicating key messages. Years of education and training make most leaders feel compelled to use all of their intellectual capabilities when speaking or writing. While this is certainly understandable, it only serves to confuse employees.

That is not to say that employees are simple people, but rather that they are inundated with information every day. What they need from leaders is clear, uncomplicated messages about where the organization is going and how they can contribute to getting there.

How does a leader go about providing the detail and context for those messages? That brings us to the final communication challenge: the use of multiple mediums.

Multiple Mediums. All too often, executives feel comfortable using just one form of communication to convey messages to the rest of the organization. Some leaders prefer live communication, either to large groups or in more intimate settings. Others feel more comfortable writing messages through e-mail or intranet postings. Still others prefer to communicate primarily to their direct reports, who are then charged with relaying messages to employees deeper in the organization.

Which of these methods is best? All of them. Relying on one or two channels of communication within an organization will guarantee that some parts of the employee population will miss key messages. This is because employees also have preferences about the way they receive information.

Engineers might prefer e-mail, salespeople often find voice mail more convenient, some employees want to hear their leaders in person, and still others are fine with an occasional update from their manager.

Although I believe that any organization needs to establish standards about how most information is disseminated, it should not do so at the expense of using all types of media to convey key messages. Even if employees could somehow be retrained to use and embrace the same forms of communication, all methods should be used because each provides an executive with a unique opportunity to reach employees and make messages clear.

For example, live communication provides opportunities for meaningful interaction and emotional context; e-mail allows for more extensive information to be received and maintained for later review; and relayed communication from an employee's manager creates an opportunity for in-depth discussion about how the message will affect people's daily jobs.

In spite of the validity of each of these mediums, there is one form of communication that I have found to be the most powerful and underused within organizations of all sizes, from twenty-five to ten thousand employees. I call it cascading communication.

After virtually every executive staff meeting that takes place in any organization, there are key decisions that have been made and issues that have been resolved, which need to be communicated. Unfortunately, the executives often leave those meetings with different interpretations of what has been decided and what is to be communicated.

I once witnessed an executive team leave a staff meeting after deciding to establish a hiring freeze throughout the company. Fifteen minutes after the meeting had ended, an e-mail message went out from the head of human resources to all employees, informing them that all job requisitions were to be placed on hold until further notice. Five minutes later, two executives from the staff meeting were in the HR VP's office, protesting that they thought the hiring freeze did not apply to their divisions.

The key is to take five minutes at the end of staff meetings and ask the question, "What do we need to communicate to our people?" After a few minutes of discussion, it will become apparent which issues need clarification and which are appropriate to communicate. Not only does this brief discussion avoid confusion among the executives themselves, it gives employees a sense that the people who head their respective departments are working together and coming to agreement on important issues.

Even when executives agree on what has been decided, there may be a wide range of viewpoints about how and how much to communicate to employees. Some executives sit down with their direct reports within a day of the meeting and fill them in on all the issues that they need to carry down to their people. Others leave voice-mail messages for their staffs, highlighting a few points. Still others communicate messages individually, on the basis of which items are relevant to which people.

This discrepancy in approach causes inevitable problems. Eventually some employees hear about executive decisions from their colleagues in other organizations, and they wonder why they aren't being kept in the loop.

How Do You Assess Your Organization for Effective Over-Communication?

This is pretty simple. Ask employees if they know why the organization exists, what its fundamental values are, what business it is in, whom its competitors are, what its strategy is, what the major goals for the year are, and who is responsible for doing what at the executive level. Then ask them how their job affects each of these areas. Blank stares and incorrect answers are good signs that more communication is needed.

DISCIPLINE FOUR: REINFORCE ORGANIZATIONAL CLARITY THROUGH HUMAN SYSTEMS

Even a company dedicated to over-communication cannot maintain organizational clarity through communication alone. It needs to build a sense of that clarity into the fabric of the organization through processes and systems that drive human behavior. The challenge lies in doing this without creating unnecessary bureaucracy.

What Does Reinforcement Through Human Systems Look Like?

An organization that uses human systems properly maintains its identity and sense of direction even during times of change. It ensures that employees will be hired, managed, rewarded, and, yes, even fired for reasons that are consistent with its organizational clarity.

There are four primary human systems that serve to institutionalize an organization's sense of clarity.

173

Discipline 4:

Reinforce Organizational Clarity Through Human Systems

Organizations sustain their health by ensuring consistency in . . .

Hiring

Managing performance

Rewards and recognition

Employee dismissal

Hiring Profiles.   One system is an interviewing and hiring profile, which is based largely on the fundamental values of an organization. Healthy organizations look for qualities in job candidates that match the values of the company. They ask behavioral questions of interviewees and probe for evidence that the candidate has the potential to fit within the organization.

After interviews have taken place, interviewers debrief with one another, paying special attention to the assessments of colleagues regarding the candidate's alignment with fundamental values. This group consultation helps organizations avoid making costly hiring mistakes, which take months and sometimes years to correct.

Contrast this to most organizations where hiring is done in a "Did you like him?" manner. Interviewers make decisions based on their gut-level reactions to candidates, and with relatively little objective criteria about whether the employee matches the organization's culture. Instead, they rely on résumé items and technical skills, which alone are poor indicators of future success.

Performance Management.   Another system that serves to reinforce an organization's clarity is its performance management process. This is the structure around which managers communicate with and direct the work of their people. It serves to help employees identify their opportunities for growth and development, and to constantly realign their work and their behaviors around the direction and values of the organization at large.

Unfortunately, most organizations place the wrong kind of emphasis on performance management, and in the process they lose the true essence of what performance management is about: communication and alignment.

There are two common misapplications that cause this to happen. Many companies make their systems too complex, requiring managers and employees to complete endless and complicated forms and numerical assessments. Too often, any sense of real management communication and coaching is lost among the instructions and requirements.

Another common problem has to do with the generic nature of many performance management systems. Too many companies purchase off-the-shelf systems designed by consulting firms whose sole purpose is to sell as many of the same forms to as many different companies as possible. It is little wonder that managers and employees alike see little value in taking time to complete them.

The best performance management systems include only essential information, and allow managers and their employees to focus on the work that must be done to ensure success.

There is relatively little emphasis on legal issues and quantitative evaluations, which often distract employees from the critical messages their managers are trying to communicate. What is more, these systems are customized to provoke meaningful discussion between managers and employees about relevant issues that they are dealing with on a daily basis.

Finally, performance management is not just about communication during employee review cycles. It is about ongoing dialogue around how employees can align their behaviors around the organization's clarity.

Rewards and Recognition.   This system has to do with the manner in which organizations reinforce behavior. Healthy organizations eliminate as much subjectivity and capriciousness as possible from the reward process by using consistent criteria for paying, recognizing, and promoting employees.

Decisions about bonuses and other compensation are based on the same criteria used in hiring and managing performance. This helps employees understand that the best way to maximize their personal rewards is to act in a way that contributes to the company's success, as defined by organizational clarity.

In addition to monetary rewards, recognition of employees is designed around the organization's values. These not only provide incentives for employees to emulate the right behaviors, but they also serve as a high-profile means of promoting the values themselves.

Finally, no one is promoted in healthy organizations unless they represent the behavioral values of the organization. Management discusses candidates for promotion not only in regard to their contribution to the bottom line but also in terms of their impact on reinforcing the clarity of the organization.

Dismissal. Healthy organizations use their values and other issues related to organizational clarity to guide their decisions about moving employees out of the company. Not only does this provide an effective means for identifying problems before they become too costly, it helps companies avoid making arbitrary decisions about an employee's suitability for remaining within the organization.

How Does an Organization Assess Itself for Human Systems?

Answering the following questions is a good start:

- Is there a process for interviewing candidates and debriefing those interviews as a team?
- Are there consistent behavioral interview questions that are asked across every department?
- Is there a consistent process for managing the performance of employees across the organization?
- Do we spend time evaluating employees' behavior versus the organization's values and goals?

- Do managers and employees willingly participate in the system?

- Is there a consistent process for determining rewards and recognition for employees?

- Is there a consistent process for evaluating promotion candidates against organizational values?

- Are there consistent criteria for removing employees from the organization?

- Are employees ever terminated because they are a poor fit within the organization's values?

While even the best organization may not be able to answer yes to each of these questions, more than a few no answers is probably an indication that better systems are needed to reinforce the organization's clarity. Organizations should continually strive to create exactly the amount of structure that is required—no more and no less.

CONCLUSION

The model described here is a holistic one; each discipline is critical to success. And because every organization is different, each will struggle with different aspects of the model.

Some leadership teams have an easier time building trust than others but lack the discipline and follow-through to put processes and systems in place. Others enjoy strategic planning and decision making but lose interest in repeatedly communicating their decisions to employees.

Whatever the case, executives must keep two things in mind if they are to make their organizations successful. First, there is nothing more important than making an organization healthy. Regardless of the temptations to dive into more heady and strategically attractive issues, extraordinary executives keep themselves focused on their organization's health.

Second, there is no substitute for discipline. No amount of intellectual prowess or personal charisma can make up for an inability to identify a few simple things and stick to them over time.

ACKNOWLEDGMENTS

Trying to adequately thank all the people who have made this book happen is a daunting task. But here goes.

Much gratitude certainly goes to my wonderful wife, Laura, for her patience, love, and strength, which I admire so much. And for loving our boys, she can never be thanked enough. I am also grateful to those twin boys, Matthew and Connor, for making it so difficult to write this book by providing me with the most delightful distractions a man could ever want.

Special thanks also go to my dear parents, my brother, and my sister, for their unconditional love and constant support.

I am extremely grateful to my staff, Amy, Tracy, John, Michele, Karen, Jeff, and Amber, for their loyalty, patience, and support. They are so much more to me than colleagues, and their commitment amazes me every day. Special thanks to Amy for keeping me moving and having confidence in me.

Thanks to Anne and Loretta for all the baby-sitting, and to Charlotte for becoming a special part of our family.

Thanks to my clients for their trust, openness, and hard work.

Thanks to my editor, Susan, and to all the passionate people at Jossey-Bass/Wiley, for their tolerance and commitment.

And most important, thank You, Lord, for everything that I have and am. Without You, I am nothing.

ABOUT THE AUTHOR

Patrick Lencioni is the author of the best-selling books *The Five Dysfunctions of a Team* and *The Five Temptations of a CEO*. In addition to his work as an author, Pat consults and speaks to thousands of people each year on topics relating to leadership, teamwork, management, and organization development. He currently serves on the National Board of Directors for the Make-A-Wish Foundation of America.

Pat is also the president of The Table Group, a San Francisco Bay Area management consulting firm that specializes in executive team development and organizational health. The Table Group offers the following professional services:

- Executive Team Workshops
- Consulting Services
- On-line Assessments
- Speaking Services

Pat lives in the San Francisco Bay Area with his wife, Laura, and their three sons, Matthew, Connor, and Casey.

To learn more about Pat and The Table Group, please visit www.tablegroup.com. If you'd like to contact Pat directly, he can be reached at 510-596-9292 or patricklencioni@tablegroup.com.

the table group